COMMERCIAL
LITIGATION

COMMERCIAL LITIGATION

Michael Waring LLB, Solicitor

2002

TABLE OF STATUTES

References are to paragraph and Appendix numbers.

TABLE OF STATUTORY INSTRUMENTS

References in the right-hand column are to paragraph and Appendix numbers.

TABLE OF ABBREVIATIONS

AA 1996	Arbitration Act 1996
ADR	alternative dispute resolution
AJA 1920	Administration of Justice Act 1920
CCR	County Court Rules 1981
CEDR	Centre for Dispute Resolution
CFA	Conditional fee agreement
CJJA 1982	Civil Jurisdiction and Judgments Act 1982
CPR 1998	Civil Procedure Rules 1998
CPS	Crown Prosecution Service
EC	European Community
ECJ	European Court of Justice
EFTA	European Free Trade Association
FJ(RE)A 1933	Foreign Judgments (Reciprocal Enforcement) Act 1933
FOSFA	Federation of Oils, Seeds and Fats Association
GAFTA	Grain and Feed Trade Association
GLO	Group Litigation Order
ICC	International Chamber of Commerce
JCT	Joint Contracts Tribunal
LA 1980	Limitation Act 1980
LCD	Lord Chancellor's Department
PD	Practice Direction
RSC	Rules of the Supreme Court 1965
TCC	Technology and Construction Court
UNCITRAL	United Nations' Commission on International Trade Law

for all the specialist lists such as the Commercial Court, the Mercantile Lists in the District Registries and the Technology and Construction Court, state that all cases commenced in those courts will automatically be allocated to the multi-track. There is no need to file allocation questionnaires in cases commenced in those courts (even if the claim is for less than £15,000).

In giving directions (which will usually be done at a case conference, rather than by post), the court will have to bear in mind its responsibilities under r 1.4(2) which include:

> '(b) identifying the issues at an early stage;
> (c) deciding promptly which issues need full investigation and trial and accordingly disposing summarily of the others;
> (d) deciding the order in which issues are to be resolved; and
> …
> (g) fixing timetables or otherwise controlling the progress of the case.'

The rules specifically say that any legal representative attending a case management conference (or a pre-trial review) must be familiar with the case (r 29.3).

However, although the court is supposed to take a pro-active role, if the parties can agree on case management proposals (including a trial date) and the court finds the parties' proposals suitable; it can give directions accordingly without the need for a hearing (r 29.4).

One of the directions which the court will give will deal with the date by which the parties must file a completed listing questionnaire. CPR 1998 do not give any guidance as to when that date should be.

Once the listings questionnaire has been filed, the court may decide to hold a pre-trial review (or may decide to cancel one which it set up when originally giving directions). The purpose of the pre-trial review is to help the court, if it has not already done so, to set a timetable for the trial and to fix the trial date (rr 29.7 and 29.8). This ties in with the exhortation in r 1.4(2) to manage cases actively by:

> '(l) giving directions to ensure that the trial of a case proceeds quickly and efficiently.'

The parties are able to vary the timetable by written agreement, as long as this does not affect the dates of the trial or for the return of the listing questionnaire. Rule 29.5 also makes it clear that, in a multi-track case, the parties will also need the leave of the court to alter the dates of the case management conference or the pre-trial review.

As will be seen elsewhere in this book, the specialist courts/lists have their own case management procedures, tailored to the type of claims that each deals with.

1.5.2 Allocating cases to the right track

When a claim is commenced for a sum of money, the claimant must specify in the claim form the amount he is claiming, or, if he is not able to put a precise figure on the value of his claim, he must state in his claim form that he expects to recover either:

(i)   more than £15,000; or
(ii) between £5,000 and £15,000; or
(iii) no more than £5,000.

If the defendant files a defence, the court sends an allocation questionnaire to every party. This gives the parties an opportunity to indicate which track they believe the case is appropriate to and why. No case (not even in the small claims track) is automatically allocated to a track by reference to the value of the claim. Among the factors the court can take into account are:

(a)   the complexity of the case;
(b)   the number of parties;
(c)   the value of any counter-claim;
(d)   the amount of oral evidence which may be required;
(e)   the circumstances of the parties;
(f)   the importance of the case to non-parties;
(g)   the nature of the remedy sought; and
(h)   the views of the parties.

The above list represents factors which can be taken into account by the court if a party is wishing to talk the case up a track (eg the claim is for £14,000 but the claimant wants the claim to be treated as a multi-track case). This list would also represent the factors to be taken into account in deciding where to allocate a case where the claimant is not seeking damages.

Given the current concern of businessmen over the costs and delays associated with litigation, it is, perhaps, unlikely that they will want to go out of their way to get a claim below £15,000 transferred into the multi-track system, thereby significantly increasing the legal costs involved. The sort of case where this might happen is where a decision will have wider implications than the dispute which is before the courts. For example, if there is a dispute about the interpretation of a standard clause used by a particular company (eg a rent review clause) and the claimant is anxious to obtain as authoritative a decision as possible on the interpretation of that clause, they may well want to argue that the case should go into the multi-track, irrespective of the value of the claim.

Where a claim with a value exceeding £15,000 is very straightforward, it is likely to be resolved more quickly and cheaply if it is allocated to the fast track. It is not possible, however, to 'allocate down' a track unless all the parties consent. Each will need to consider carefully whether a one-day trial and the restrictions which the court is likely to impose on the evidence to be allowed at trial will adversely affect their case. Interestingly, r 16.3(7) says that:

> 'The statement of value in the claim form does not limit the power of the court to give judgment for the amount which it finds the claimant is entitled to.'

This suggests that it is possible for a claimant to commence proceedings in the fast track by putting in the claim form a statement of value that he reasonably expects to recover no more than £15,000, and then ask at trial for damages in excess of £15,000. Depending on the circumstances, the defendant might seek to persuade the court that it would not be appropriate to award damages in excess of £15,000. Where it becomes clear prior to trial that the value of the claim has increased to over £15,000, both parties should consider whether either wishes to apply to the court for the case to be re-allocated to the multi-track, on the basis that the way in which the case will be resolved on the fast track is no longer appropriate. It is likely that, the earlier in the litigation process such an application is made, the greater the chance of it succeeding.

risk of inconsistent judgments on related matters. On the other hand, there is a limit to what can appropriately be dealt with in a single action. The purpose of the court rules is to enable the court to strike a sensible balance.

2.4.1 Causes of action

It is not at all unusual for a number of causes of action to be dealt with in a single action. Under r 7.3 of CPR 1998, the claimant may use a single claim form to start all claims which can be conveniently disposed of in the same proceedings.

However, the claimant may run into difficulties if he wishes to introduce a new cause of action after he has served his particulars of claim. He cannot amend the particulars of claim without obtaining either the written consent of all the other parties or the permission of the court. Broadly, the court is likely to allow the amendment provided the new cause of action can conveniently be dealt with as part of the original proceedings. Important factors are whether the amendment would necessitate an alteration in the arrangements for trial and whether it is fair for the defendant to face a new claim given the stage the proceedings have reached.

More stringent considerations apply where the claimant is seeking to introduce a cause of action after the expiry of the limitation period. The court has a discretion to allow the amendment if the new claim arises out of the same facts or substantially the same facts as an existing claim.

> *Example*
> C sues D for breach of contract, issuing the claim form on 1 March. In December, he decides he also wishes to bring a claim against D for negligence, but the limitation period for this expired in June. If C issued a separate claim form, D would have an impregnable defence. If, however, he is allowed to amend his original claim form and particulars of claim, the negligence claim will be treated as having been made on the date the original claim form was issued. The court may only allow the amendment if the negligence and contract claims arise out of the same or substantially the same facts.

2.4.2 Addition, substitution and removal of parties

Part 19 of CPR 1998 states that, once a claim form has been served, the court's permission is required to remove, add or substitute a party. An application to the court may be made, either by an existing party or by a person who wishes to be added as a party.

Adding a party

The court may add a new party to the proceedings if:

- it is desirable for resolving the matters in dispute; or
- there is an issue involving the new party and an existing party which is connected to the matters in dispute in the existing proceedings and it is desirable to add the new party so that the court can resolve that issue.

A party cannot be added as a claimant unless their written consent has been filed at court. The court may, however, require such a party to be joined as a defendant.

Removing a party

The court can order any person to cease to be a party to proceedings if it is not desirable that they should be one.

Substituting a party

The court may order the substitution of one party for another provided this is desirable and the original party's interest or liability has passed to the new party.

Where the court makes an order removing, substituting or adding a party, it may also make any consequential directions that are necessary, such as the serving of relevant documents on a new party.

Limitation

Special considerations apply where a party wishes to add or substitute after the expiration of a limitation period.

The court may add or substitute a party if the relevant limitation period was current when the proceedings were started and the addition or substitution is necessary. Rule 19.5(3) provides that it is only necessary if the court is satisfied that:

- the new party is to be substituted for a party who was named in the claim form in mistake for the new party; or
- the claim cannot properly be carried on by or against the original party unless the addition or substitution takes place; or
- the original party has died or is the subject of a bankruptcy order and his interest or liability has passed to the new party.

There are further provisions relating to personal injuries claims which are not within the scope of this book.

2.4.3 Consolidation

As part of its general management powers (see further **2.8.1**), the court may direct that two or more actions shall be consolidated into a single action (r 3.1(2)(g)). The purpose of consolidation is to save costs by avoiding unnecessary duplication of work during the interim stages and by holding a single trial. Alternatively, the court may leave the actions as separate proceedings but order that they be tried together (r 3.1(2)(h)).

In both cases, the court can make the order on its own initiative or on the application of a party. The claims must be pending in the same court, but where they have been started in different courts, they can be transferred so that the order can be made.

2.4.4 Multi-party actions

This is intended only as a brief introduction to this topic. The solicitor handling a case should consider at the outset of a dispute whether a multi-party approach is appropriate. If so, specialist advice, or at least further research into CPR 1998 will be required.

Part 19 identifies two categories of proceedings that can be described as multi-party:

- proceedings taken or defended by representative parties; and
- group litigation.

Chapter 3

THE COMMERCIAL COURT

3.1 INTRODUCTION

As stated in **1.1**, much commercial litigation is conducted in the Commercial Court. This chapter explains the role of the Commercial Court and its special practices and procedures.

3.1.1 The court

The Commercial Court is part of the Admiralty and Commercial Registry which is itself part of the Queen's Bench Division of the High Court. The Commercial Court was established in 1895 to provide a court which was familiar with commercial disputes and which would have procedures to enable such disputes to be resolved quickly and efficiently. It was restructured in its present form in 1970.

Part of QBD — High Ct.

The Commercial Court provides a specialised service for businessmen. The judges of the Commercial Court are specifically assigned to that court. They practised in the Commercial Court before they became judges and are experts in the types of case dealt with by the Commercial Court. Although the court can be, and is, used for relatively straightforward matters, it also attracts cases which are highly complex and involve vast sums of money. Much of the court's specialised practice arises from the need to prevent these 'heavy' cases from becoming 'bogged down' by the weight of the evidence. Slow progress to a lengthy trial is discouraged.

Over 75% of cases in the Commercial Court have at least one party based outside the jurisdiction and, in some years, half of the cases proceeding in the Commercial Court have parties on both sides who are from outside the jurisdiction.

3.1.2 The Guide to Commercial Court Practice

The CPR 1998 apply to cases in the Commercial Court. However, they have to be interpreted in the light of any specialist Practice Directions relating to the Commercial Court, and particularly in the light of the 5th edition of the *Guide to Commercial Court Practice* ('the Guide').

"The Guide"

The Guide is prepared by the Commercial Court Committee ('the Committee'). The Committee is made up of judges and representatives of practitioners and users of the court. It receives and discusses suggestions for improving Commercial Court practice and makes recommendations to the judges, who approve the final version of the Guide.

The 5th edition of the Guide has 15 detailed sections dealing with the various stages of a Commercial Court action. It also has 20 appendices dealing with various aspects of litigation in the Commercial Court. It runs to 189 pages and what follows can only be a basic summary of practice in the Commercial Court. Anyone handling a Commercial Court action who does not use the information in the Guide will have great difficulty in presenting his case and may find himself incurring costs penalties. The Guide can be found online at the Court Service website.

The Introduction to the Guide deals with the relationship between the Guide and CPR 1998. It says:

> 'The Civil Procedure Rules apply to cases in the Commercial List subject to the provisions of this Guide. This Guide adapts some of the Civil Procedure Rules, and puts others in a particular context, in order that the special demands of the work of the Court can be met. To the same end it also introduces some further procedural requirements not found in the Civil Procedure Rules.'

and

> 'This Guide is not a substitute for the Civil Procedure Rules, and does not attempt to cover all procedural points. It is not a litigation hand-book nor a blue-print to which all litigation must unthinkingly conform. It rather seeks to provide a modern and flexible framework within which litigation in the Commercial Court can be conducted with efficiency and in the interests of justice.'

To summarise, litigation in the Commercial Court is largely conducted under the provisions of the Guide and, where this conflicts with CPR 1998, the Commercial Court will follow the provisions of the Guide, subject to the need to meet the overriding objective.

The Guide does not purport to cover every aspect of civil procedure. Appendix 1 to the Guide contains a useful schedule indicating the extent to which the normal Practice Directions which supplement each part of CPR 1998 will apply in the Commercial Court.

This chapter will concentrate on those aspects of practice in the Commercial Court which depart from the norm of CPR 1998. Unless stated to the contrary, readers may assume that CPR 1998 have not been affected by the Guide.

3.1.3 The practice of the court

Proceedings in the Commercial Court follow the same order of events as other court actions. All the usual interim steps (eg payment into court, disclosure, interim payments, etc) can be taken in the Commercial Court in the same way as in any other case. This chapter simply highlights the extent to which proceedings in the Commercial Court differ from other civil proceedings.

The court's practice places great emphasis on co-operation between the parties' lawyers (many of whom are specialists in commercial litigation). They are expected to show a sense of realism in their handling of the case. This applies to dealings (including correspondence) between the parties' legal representatives, as well as to their dealings with the court. For example, the court encourages them to give advance disclosure of information and to provide written summaries which can be read by the judge before the hearing of an application or during the course of a trial in order to save time.

The practices of the Commercial Court have been the model for many of the changes introduced by CPR 1998.

3.5.7 Security for costs

Where the defendant (or Part 20 defendant) intends to apply for security for costs (see Chapter 14), he should do so no later than the case management conference. Guidance is provided by Appendix 18 to the Guide. This states that any delay which is prejudicial to the claimant or to the administration of justice will probably cause the application to fail. Similarly, if the court forms the view that the application is motivated by a desire to harass the defendant, it is likely to be refused.

The Commercial Court is reluctant to investigate the merits when considering the application. The merits will only be taken into account in cases where it is clear without any detailed examination of the facts or the law that the claim is certain or almost certain to fail.

As a condition of the grant of security, the defendant may be required to give an undertaking to the court to comply with any subsequent order to compensate the claimant for any loss suffered as a result of giving security. This would be appropriate where no costs order was ultimately made in the defendant's favour.

Where security is granted, this will usually be on the basis that, if the claimant fails to comply with the order, it is for the defendant to apply to the court for an order to stay the proceedings or to strike out the particulars of claim. Unless the defendant does so, the case will continue in accordance with the pre-trial timetable. The aim is to prevent any unnecessary delay in the proceedings pending a decision by the court about the claimant's default.

3.5.8 ADR

Paragraph D7.14 of the Guide indicates that the court will consider applications for an adjournment of the case at the case management conference stage to enable the parties to negotiate a settlement or to use some form of ADR. The parties can use the case management information sheet to indicate that such an adjournment may be appropriate.

If the court does adjourn the case and *all* parties want an extension to the adjournment, one of the parties should write to the court before the end of the adjournment period confirming that all parties consent to the further adjournment. The letter should also explain what steps are being taken to settle the case and identify any mediator or other third party who is seeking to help the parties to settle the case. As under CPR 1998, any further adjournment is likely to be for no more than 4 weeks, but the court can then grant further adjournments if it sees fit.

The Guide then goes on to say:

> 'Alternatively, an ADR order may be made without an order adjourning the case. The parties should give careful consideration to the possibilities of fitting ADR into the pre-trial timetable without the need for any or much delay to it.'

3.5.9 The pre-trial timetable

This will include a progress monitoring date (see below) and a fixed date for the trial, which the parties will normally agree with the Clerk to the Commercial Court shortly after the case management conference. A standard form of pre-trial timetable is set out in Appendix C at the end of this book.

The parties can agree minor variations to the timetable as long as the overall structure is not affected and the variation will not affect the trial date or the progress monitoring date.

If more significant variations to the timetable are needed, the parties should apply to the court for a further case management conference rather than waiting until the progress monitoring date.

3.5.10 Special cases

There are minor variations to the rules on case management conferences for Part 8 and Part 20 claims in paras D7.20 *et seq* of the Guide. Students need not concern themselves with this level of detail.

3.5.11 Progress monitoring

At the case management conference, the court will fix a progress monitoring date which will usually be after the time for exchanging witness statements and expert reports has expired.

The parties must serve and file a progress monitoring information sheet at least 3 days before the progress monitoring date. This will tell the court:

(a) the extent to which they have been able to comply with the pre-trial timetable to date; and
(b) whether they will be ready for trial on time and, if not, when they will be ready for trial.

A standard form of progress monitoring sheet appears in Appendix D at the end of this book.

3.5.12 Pre-trial checklist

If the parties, in their progress monitoring information sheets, indicate that they will be ready for trial on time, they must, within 7 days after the progress monitoring date, file and serve a completed pre-trial checklist. The court will then confirm the trial date.

A standard form of pre-trial checklist appears in Appendix E at the end of this book.

3.5.13 Reconvening the case management conference

If the progress monitoring information sheets show that one or more of the parties will not, or may not, be ready in time for the trial, the court can reconvene the case management conference. It can rewrite the pre-trial timetable by giving further directions and can make any appropriate orders for costs. It can also stipulate that a statement of case will be automatically struck out unless the party concerned complies with certain directions by certain specified dates.

A defendant who wishes to raise a Part 20 claim in a Part 8 case will always need the permission of the court to do so. If the court grants permission it will give directions regarding the conduct of the Part 20 claim.

A defendant who believes that the Part 8 procedure is not appropriate should state his objections and the reasons for them when he files his acknowledgment of service. The court will then have to give directions as to the future management of the case, and these could include an order that the claim continue as if the Part 8 procedure had not been used.

4.3 FURTHER READING

The Guide to Chancery Court Practice (available from the Court Service's website at www.courtservice.gov.uk and in hard copy in vol 2 of *Civil Procedure* (Sweet & Maxwell, 2001).

Chapman and Counsell *Chancery Practice and Procedure* (Jordans, 2001).

injunction until B is well established in business, when the court will uphold the 'status quo' by refusing an injunction.

A couple of cases may help to illustrate the court's approach in deciding the balance of convenience. In *Dalgety Spillers Foods Ltd v Food Brokers Ltd* [1994] FSR 504, the defendants had plans to market a range of food products in competition with the claimants' established range of food products. They were aware that the claimants might try to prevent this by a passing off action and that the claimants might seek an injunction restraining them from marketing this particular product. The defendants therefore wrote to the claimants in October 1992 advising the claimants of their plans. The claimants acknowledged this letter but took no further action. The defendants put their products on the market in September 1993. The claimants then issued a claim form alleging 'passing off' and applied for an injunction. The court refused the injunction because the claimants' failure to respond to the original letter had caused the defendants to expend time, trouble and cost which they might not have incurred if the claimants had given an earlier indication of their objections.

In *News Group Newspapers Ltd v Mirror Group Newspapers Ltd* [1989] FSR 126, the defendants had advertised their newspaper by using the 'masthead' of *The Sun* which was a newspaper published by the claimants. The claimants sought an injunction to prevent this and succeeded because the injunction would cause little or no harm to the defendants, whereas the claimants could suffer significant harm if the defendants were allowed to continue what they were doing.

Finally, although the whole object of the *American Cyanamid* guidelines is to avoid a detailed investigation of the facts at this stage, if the above approach does not produce a solution, the court can be influenced by the fact that one party seems clearly to have the stronger case. Under this guideline, the court will only take into account the relative strengths of a party's case if there is no significant difference in the harm each party will suffer if the application goes against them, and the witness statements clearly show that one party has a disproportionately stronger case.

5.5.4 Special factors

When setting out the *American Cyanamid* guidelines, Lord Diplock stated:

> 'I would reiterate that, in addition to those to which I have referred, there may be many other special factors to be taken into consideration in the particular circumstances of individual cases.'

There is no definition of what may amount to special factors, but case-law since *American Cyanamid* gives various examples, such as injunctions to thwart winding up petitions and defamation. Other special cases are considered in **5.6**.

5.5.5 Approach of the courts in practice

Cases since *American Cyanamid* have stressed that the guidelines 'must never be used as a rule of thumb, let alone as a straitjacket' (Kerr LJ in *Cambridge Nutrition Ltd v BBC* [1990] 3 All ER 523). The courts are mindful that this is a flexible remedy and it is a matter of discretion, taking into account all the facts. In his judgment in *Series 5 Software v Clarke* [1996] 1 All ER 853, Laddie J discussed whether the courts are just paying 'lip-service' to *American Cyanamid* as, in practice, they still seem to consider the strengths of the parties' cases, when reaching their decision. It was Laddie J's view that the House of Lords in *American Cyanamid* was trying to stop mini-trials, with detailed analysis of evidence at the interim injunction stage. However, this did not prevent the courts from looking at the strengths of a party's case at this stage, and this certainly seemed to be the practice prior to *American Cyanamid*. In *Series 5 Software*, Laddie J acknowledged that the courts should not try and solve complex issues of law and fact at this interim stage. Nevertheless, he suggested that if it is apparent from the material available that one party's case is stronger than another, this should not be ignored.

5.6 INJUNCTIONS WHERE *AMERICAN CYANAMID* DOES NOT APPLY

In some special cases, set out below, the courts have varied or not applied the *American Cyanamid* guidelines.

5.6.1 There is unlikely to be a trial

The *American Cyanamid* approach assumes that the case will proceed to trial and that the claimant will either win his case and get a final injunction or will lose and the defendant will be compensated for the harm caused by the earlier interim injunction. There are many cases, however, where the result of the interim application will be decisive and the action will never go to trial. The case of *Fulwell v Bragg* (1983) *The Times*, January 6 is an example. A firm of solicitors had expelled one of its partners. He considered that his expulsion was improper and wanted to persuade former clients of the firm to take their business away from the firm and to deal with him. He sought an order requiring the firm to allow him to do this. It was common ground that, whether an injunction was granted or refused, the matter would end there. The court, therefore, felt obliged to do what it could to investigate the merits of both parties' claims.

This illustrates that where there is unlikely to be a trial, the *American Cyanamid* guidelines do not apply and the claimant must show that he is likely to succeed at trial before an injunction will be granted.

5.6.2 Applications to prevent court proceedings

If a claimant wants to prevent someone from bringing proceedings in this country, he will have to show that those proceedings will be an abuse of process (*Bryanstone Finance Ltd v De Vries (No 2)* [1976] Ch 63).

If a claimant wants an order preventing someone from taking legal proceedings in another country, he must establish:

(1) that there are equivalent proceedings which could be taken in this country; and
(2) that the English proceedings would be much less vexatious and oppressive than the foreign proceedings (*Arab Monetary Fund v Hashim (No 6)* (1992) *The Times*, July 24).

As stated in *Bankers Trust Co and Another v PT Jakarta International Hotels & Development* [1999] 1 All ER 785:

'Similarly the courts will enforce an arbitration agreement governed by English law by granting an injunction restraining the respondent from bringing foreign proceedings in breach of that agreement.'

5.6.3 Public interest

The courts will usually grant an injunction preventing publication of confidential information if it is in the public interest that confidentiality should be preserved. They do recognise, however, that there are cases where the public interest requires the truth to be revealed. Two examples of cases where an injunction against publication was refused on this ground are *Lion Laboratories Ltd v Evans* [1985] QB 526 (former employee seeking to disclose information about the reliability of a breath-test machine) and *In re a Company's Application* [1989] Ch 477 (reports of alleged infringements of the tax laws and the Financial Services Act 1986). In such public interest cases, the courts are not afraid to investigate the merits of the case before deciding whether to grant an injunction.

5.6.4 Mandatory injunctions

It is very difficult to get a mandatory interim injunction since the court usually requires clear evidence that the claimant is likely to succeed at trial and the *American Cyanamid* guidelines do not apply. Thus, in *Jakeman v South West Thames Regional Health Authority* [1990] IRLR 62, an employee failed to obtain an interim order for the payment of allegedly withheld wages.

However, the presumption against granting interim mandatory injunctions can be overridden if refusal of an injunction would clearly cause undue hardship. For example, in *Films Rover International Ltd v Cannon Film Sales Ltd* [1986] 3 All ER 772, the defendant was the claimant's only supplier and the claimant would go out of business if an injunction was not granted. In *Nikitenko v Leboeuf Lamb Greene & MacRea* (1996) *The Times*, January 26, the court ordered the defendant to disclose documents to the claimant even though it was not sure that the claimant was entitled to see those documents. It did so because disclosure was unlikely to harm the defendant, whereas if the claimant was entitled to see the documents it was vital that he do so now. The case is, however, exceptional. The balance of convenience is generally not a relevant issue when considering an interim mandatory injunction.

Mandatory injunctions should not be confused with orders pursuant to s 99 of the Copyright Designs and Patents Act 1988 for delivery up of copies or articles where the claimant alleges breach of copyright.

5.6.5 Other cases

Freezing injunctions and search orders

The *American Cyanamid* principles are not appropriate for freezing injunctions and search orders. These are dealt with in Chapters 7 and 8.

Land

The court will always grant an injunction to restrain breach of an enforceable restrictive covenant relating to land. As the defendant has already promised not to behave in a particular way, the court will enforce his promise (*Hampstead & Suburban Properties Ltd v Diomedous* [1969] 1 Ch 248). Similarly, if the defendant is clearly trespassing on the claimant's land, the claimant will usually be entitled to an injunction to restrain the trespass even if the trespass did not harm him.

Trade disputes

Section 221(2) of the Trade Union and Labour Relations (Consolidation) Act 1992 specifically states that, where an injunction is sought against a defendant who claims that he is acting 'in contemplation or furtherance of a trade dispute' (as defined by the Act), the court must 'have regard to the likelihood of [the defendant's] succeeding at the trial'. The defendant may raise the defence of immunity from certain tort liabilities or peaceful picketing under ss 219 and 220 of the Trade Union and Labour Relations (Consolidation) Act 1992 respectively. If the defence is likely to succeed at the trial, an injunction will be refused unless this would be disastrous for the claimant or other people. In such a case the defendant will have to show that his defence is almost certain to succeed before an injunction will be refused (*NWL Ltd v Woods* [1979] 3 All ER 614).

5.7 INJUNCTIONS WITHOUT NOTICE

Orders are made without notice if the matter is so urgent that the claimant does not have time to tell the defendant that he intends to seek an injunction. They are also made if secrecy is needed because, if the defendant learns of the claimant's plans, he will try to cause irreparable harm to the claimant before the claimant gets an injunction.

> *Example*
> B has just been sacked by A. B is about to set up in business in competition with A. A has evidence that B is going to use confidential information belonging to A to compete with A. A also has evidence that B will conceal or destroy any confidential papers if he knows that A is taking court proceedings. A would be entitled to apply for an injunction without notice restraining B from using such information.

To proceed without notice, the claimant must also show that he has a strong enough case to justify the court not hearing the defendant's case. This is a departure from the rules of natural justice that all parties should be heard. Therefore, in the interests of fairness, the claimant must disclose all relevant facts, including any matters favourable to the defendant. Failure to do this will result in the injunction being set aside with orders for costs against the claimant who may also have to pay damages to the defendant for any harm caused by the injunction.

Section 221(1) of the Trade Union and Labour Relations (Consolidation) Act 1992 prohibits injunctions without notice where the defendant is likely to claim that he is acting 'in contemplation or furtherance of a trade dispute' (as defined by the Act) unless 'satisfied that all steps which in the circumstances were reasonable have been taken with a view to securing that notice of the application and an opportunity of being heard ... have been given to that party'.

5.8 UNDERTAKINGS IN PLACE OF AN INJUNCTION

A defendant who: (i) denies the claimant's allegations; or (ii) is prepared to wait until the trial before challenging them; or (iii) concedes that the claimant is likely to succeed, may save costs by giving an undertaking to the court to avoid the need for an injunction. This will usually be in the same terms as the injunction the claimant is seeking. Such an undertaking has the same effect as an injunction and non-compliance is punishable as a contempt of court.

Sometimes the defendant is not prepared to give an undertaking until the court has found in the claimant's favour at an interim hearing. He will then offer an undertaking (which may be 'without prejudice to an appeal') so that, at any subsequent hearing, he is not at a psychological disadvantage in being regarded by the judge as a person who has had to be restrained by an injunction.

5.9 VARYING AND SETTING ASIDE INJUNCTIONS

As mentioned in **5.2**, an interim injunction on notice lasts 'until trial or further order'. It will usually contain a clause giving either party liberty to apply to vary or set aside the order. Even if it does not expressly do so, either party can apply to vary or set aside the order if circumstances change. The defendant is more likely to apply for this than the claimant. For example, he may do this because the burden of the injunction has become too onerous, as in *Jordan v Norfolk County Council* [1994] 1 WLR 1353. In that case, the defendant council had caused damage to the claimant's land by an admitted trespass. The claimant obtained an injunction requiring the defendant to make good that damage. Everyone assumed that this would cost about £12,000. The defendant then learned that the cost of complying with the order would be over £250,000. The claimant's land was worth only £25,000. The court varied the injunction.

A defendant may combine an application to set aside the injunction with an application to dismiss the claimant's action for want of prosecution. This is appropriate if the claimant does not proceed with his case with all proper speed. For instance, he may try and delay proceedings because he realises there is a risk that he will be unsuccessful at trial and fail to obtain a permanent injunction. By delaying, he ensures that he benefits from the interim injunction for as long as possible prior to trial.

A defendant may also apply to vary or set aside an undertaking. However, it is more difficult to do this because the defendant gave the original undertaking voluntarily. In *Chanel Ltd v F W Woolworth* [1981] 1 WLR 485, the Court of Appeal held that the defendants could only vary their undertaking if there had been a significant change of circumstances or they had become aware of new facts which they could not possibly have known about when they gave their undertaking.

As regards orders without notice, these can also be varied or set aside by the defendant, either on the return date fixed by the order, or on the defendant's application at any time (see **5.2**). Non-disclosure of material facts by the claimant is often the principal ground for setting aside an order without notice. Thus, on an application to set aside an interim prohibitory injunction on this ground, the court will again apply the *American Cyanamid* guidelines and decide whether, in the light

When the court grants an application for an injunction made without notice, the applicant will have to serve the injunction on the respondent. At the same time, unless the court directs otherwise, he must serve the application and the supporting evidence on all respondents against whom the order was sought (even if it was not made in respect of all of those respondents).

He should also provide full notes of the hearing (*Interoute Telecommunications (UK) Ltd v Fashion Group Ltd* (1999) *The Times*, November 10).

When the order has been served on the respondent, he can apply to the court to set aside or vary the injunction. He will normally have to do so within 7 days of the order being served on him. The order will contain a statement reminding the respondent of this right and the time-limit (r 23.9(3)).

The usual ground for applying to set aside an injunction made without notice is likely to be that the applicant did not disclose all relevant information to the court. This is dealt with in more detail in Chapter 7.

Applications outside normal court hours

Cases of extreme urgency can be dealt with by telephone. The detail is set out in para 4.5 of PD 25:

(a) the judge is likely to require a draft order to be faxed to him/her;
(b) the application notice and supporting evidence must be filed in court on the same day (or the next working day if so ordered) together with two copies of the order for sealing;
(c) the applicant must be legally represented.

If the court office is closed, the claimant's solicitor will first have to contact the court's security officer. He or she will put the claimant's solicitor in contact with the duty judge's clerk who will then, if they consider it appropriate, give the claimant's solicitor a telephone number for the duty judge.

Costs

A judge who hears an application for an injunction without notice is unlikely to make any final order for the payment of costs. He or she is likely to leave the issue of costs open until the return date.

Contents of the order without notice

An injunction made without notice will, in addition to the usual undertaking as to damages, contain the following undertakings:

(a) an undertaking by the applicant to serve the application notice, supporting evidence, and the injunction on the respondent as soon as practicable;
(b) (where relevant) an undertaking to file the application notice and pay the court fee on the same day or the next working day; and
(c) (where relevant) an undertaking to issue the claim form and pay the court fee on the same day or the next working day (unless the court gives other directions for the commencement of the claim).

It will also contain a return date, which is a hearing where the respondent will have the opportunity to argue that the injunction should be set aside.

A suggested form of injunction without notice is set out in Appendix K to this book.

6.3 SERVICE

The rules relating to service and enforcement of injunctions are contained in the re-enacted provisions of Ord 45 of RSC. Ord 45, r 7(2) states that an injunction must be served personally on the defendant before the claimant can take any steps to enforce it. It also states that a mandatory injunction must be served on the defendant before the time stated in the injunction for compliance with the order has expired.

Rule 6.9 of CPR 1998 does give the court power to dispense with service, and r 6.8 does enable the court to authorise service by some alternative method if the usual methods are impracticable. The court is only likely to exercise these powers in injunction cases when the defendant is trying to evade service.

RSC Ord 45, r 7(6) (reproduced in CPR 1998, Sch 1) allows the court to enforce a purely prohibitory injunction before it has been served if the respondent was present when the injunction was granted or has subsequently been informed of its terms (eg by telephone).

6.4 ENFORCEMENT

CPR 1998 do not deal with enforcement, which will continue for the time being to be dealt with under the re-enacted RSC.

6.4.1 Methods of enforcement

Injunctions are strictly enforced. Even if the respondent believed that his actions did not break the injunction, he will be in contempt of court if the court rules that he has broken the injunction (*In re Mileage Conference Group of the Tyre Manufacturers' Conference Ltd's Agreement* [1966] 1 WLR 1137).

If the respondent does not comply with the injunction then, under RSC Ord 45, r 5(1), the two principal methods of enforcing an injunction are sequestration (seizure of property) and committal to prison. Alternatively, the court may: (i) impose a fine; or (ii) take security to be of good behaviour; or (iii) under RSC Ord 45, r 8, order that the acts required to remedy the breach be done by some person appointed by the court, at the respondent's expense. The court's role is to ensure future compliance. Punishment is a secondary consideration. As a result, the first enforcement order is often suspended. It will only affect the respondent if he breaks the injunction again.

Sequestration is usually used where the respondent is a limited company or an unincorporated association like a trade union (although it can also be used against the property of any director or officer of such an organisation if they were parties to the breach). If the court grants leave for a writ of sequestration to be issued, it appoints four commissioners to handle the respondent's finances and to extract a financial penalty for breaking the injunction. The amount of the penalty is fixed by the court. Companies may be vicariously liable for the acts of their employees (*Re Supply of Ready Mixed Concrete (No 2)* [1994] 3 WLR 1249).

Individual respondents can be committed to prison for contempt of court. This penalty is also used against the individual officers of a defendant company who were injunction will automatically lapse if he does not provide the guarantee within the time specified in his undertaking.

The claimant also undertakes to serve the claim form on the defendant along with the order. The words in square brackets will be included where, as is often the case, the order has been obtained before issuing the claim form. This undertaking effectively means that the injunction cannot be served until a claim form has been issued. If that is not possible, the claimant's lawyers must try to persuade the court to accept a variation of the standard undertaking.

The fourth undertaking will be needed wherever the claimant has not had time to complete all the usual formalities regarding evidence before applying for an injunction. As undertaking (5) shows, the evidence is served with the injunction along with notice of the return date (see **7.6.4**).

As the third parties who have possession or control of the defendant's property are required to police the order, they will obviously need copies of it. The sixth undertaking deals with this.

In undertaking (7), the claimant promises to reimburse the third parties (eg, the bank with whom the defendant holds an account) for the expenses they incur in complying with the injunction. In practice, the third parties will usually pass on these costs to their customer (the defendant). If the defendant cannot meet these costs, the claimant will have to meet the bill which will cover both legal and administrative costs.

Finally, the claimant has to undertake to inform all third parties affected by the injunction if it lapses, for example because the claimant fails to provide the bank guarantee or the defendant provides security (see below).

7.6 THE TERMS OF THE ORDER

PD 25 – Interim Injunctions – contains a suggested form of freezing injunction. This is reproduced in Appendix L to this book. It will need to be amended and added to, depending on the facts of the individual case. However, an injunction omitting important terms may be set aside (*The Bank v A Ltd and Others* (2000) *The Times*, July 18). The order must also contain the usual penal notice.

The Notice to the Respondent at the beginning of the order explains the effect of the order and warns the defendant of the consequences of breaking the injunction. It advises him to take legal advice and that he may be able to get the order varied or set aside.

7.6.1 Freezing the assets

Clause 1 is the principal part of the order. It prevents the defendant from dealing with his property in any way. The order should, if possible, identify the property in question because this helps the third parties to police the order. However, it is not always practicable to give such detail because the claimant often does not have the necessary knowledge. If joint property is to be frozen, specific reference must be made to the jointly owned assets.

If a defendant holds assets as a bare trustee, so that he has no beneficial interest in them, then such assets will not come within the scope of a standard form freezing injunction. However, in *Federal Bank of the Middle East v Hadkinson* [2000] 1 WLR 1695 the Court of Appeal held that orders made in more specific terms might cover bank accounts in which a defendant had no beneficial interest but which were in his name and under his control.

Clause 2 of the order specifies the value of the property to which it applies (ie the amount sought by the claimant). If the defendant has more property than the amount specified in the order, he remains free to use the surplus.

TDK Tape Distributor (UK) Ltd v Videochoice Ltd [1985] 3 All ER 345 confirms that the order is not limited to property owned by the defendant when the order was made. The order operates like a floating charge, in the sense that any property the defendant subsequently acquires is still subject to the terms of the order (although it does not give the claimant priority as a creditor – see **7.1**). Indeed, *Bank Mellat v Kazmi* [1989] 1 QB 541 decided that a defendant subject to a freezing injunction would be in breach of the order if he forgave payment of a debt due to him.

If the case does go to trial and the claimant wins, he will want to continue the injunction until he has been able to enforce his judgment. *Orwell Steel (Erection and Fabrication) Ltd v Ashphalt and Tarmac (UK) Ltd* [1984] 1 WLR 1097 confirms that the trial judge has jurisdiction to continue the order in this way after judgment (see also r 25.2(1)(b) of CPR 1998).

7.6.2 Exceptions to the order

Although clause 1 of the order prevents the defendant from dealing with his property, a defendant still needs money to meet his day-to-day living expenses. The exceptions to the order set out in clause 3 deal with this by allowing him to withdraw a specified weekly sum to meet these expenses and other recurrent bills. According to *PCW (Underwriting Agencies) Ltd v Dixon* [1983] 2 All ER 158, the amount should be a reasonable sum based on the defendant's usual life-style. The exceptions also allow a specified weekly amount for business expenses and payment of legal costs. In return, the defendant has to tell the claimant's solicitors where he is getting the money from.

If the defendant is 'a smaller business', the order should usually give unqualified permission to meet ordinary trade debts. Paragraph 2 of the exceptions does this. Unfortunately, there is no definition of a 'smaller business'. As a rough guide, private companies are more likely to be 'smaller businesses' than public companies.

Paragraph 3 of the exceptions enables the parties to agree in writing that the defendant can incur additional expenditure. If the parties cannot agree, the defendant can ask the court for permission to incur the additional expenditure.

The last exception gives the defendant the opportunity to bring the injunction to an end by providing security for the amount applied for by the claimant, for example by a payment into court.

7.6.3 Disclosure

Clause 4 of the order requires the defendant to reveal what property he owns within the jurisdiction. The defendant must serve an affidavit confirming this information, usually within 7 days. Nevertheless, this clause also informs the defendant that, in cases where the privilege against self-incrimination applies, he may be entitled to

7.11 SUMMARY

A freezing injunction is an exceptional remedy which enables the claimant to prevent the defendant from dealing with some of his property until the claimant's action comes to trial. The court will grant this injunction only where the claimant can demonstrate that:

(1) he has a good arguable claim; and

(2) the defendant has property within the jurisdiction which he may deal with, otherwise than in the ordinary course of business, and in a manner which will make it more difficult for the claimant to enforce any judgment he may later obtain.

The claimant will apply without notice for the injunction. He will have to give undertakings to protect the position of the defendant and the third parties who have possession of the defendant's property.

The injunction prevents the defendant from dealing with his property up to a specified value and will usually require him to disclose what assets he has and where they are. It will also, among other things, allow him to spend a certain amount of money for ordinary living expenses, legal costs and paying his business debts.

If the claimant is accusing the defendant of criminal behaviour, the defendant may be able to rely on the privilege against self-incrimination to avoid revealing information about his assets.

If the claimant has failed to reveal information relevant to the case, the injunction may be set aside and the claimant could then have to pay compensation to the defendant under the usual undertaking as to damages.

The court in very exceptional circumstances grants freezing injunctions where the bulk of the defendant's property is outside the jurisdiction.

7.12 FURTHER READING

Goldrein and Wilkinson *Commercial Litigation – Pre-emptive Remedies* 3rd edn (Sweet & Maxwell, 1996).

Chapter 8

SEARCH ORDERS

8.1 INTRODUCTION

This chapter explains how a claimant can get an order which requests the defendant to allow the claimant to enter and search the defendant's premises for property belonging to the claimant or for evidence that the defendant has been harming the claimant. If the defendant does not comply, he may be committed to prison for contempt of court.

This chapter also explains the facts the claimant must prove to get such an order and the dangers to the claimant in seeking such an order. The obligations created by the order are set out at **8.5**, which refers to the standard form search order contained in PD 25 – Interim Injunctions, set out in Appendix M. It also deals with the undertakings the claimant and other people involved in the execution of the order have to give to the court.

The chapter concludes with some tips on the advice the defendant's solicitor should give to his or her client, and some practical points which might be of relevance to one or other of the parties.

8.2 THE NATURE OF THE ORDER

The court's power to grant a search order was established by the Court of Appeal in *Anton Piller KG v Manufacturing Processes Ltd and Others* [1976] Ch 55. In the same way as freezing injunctions used to be called *Mareva* injunctions, search orders used to be called *Anton Piller* orders and readers should bear this in mind when reading pre-1999 cases. The court now has statutory authority to make such an order pursuant to s 7 of the Civil Procedure Act 1997.

A search order requires the defendant to allow the claimant's named representatives to enter and search the defendant's premises specified in the order. The claimant, however, is not permitted to use force to enter the defendant's premises (*Anton Piller KG v Manufacturing Processes Ltd and Others* [1976] Ch 55).

The order is used to recover property belonging to the claimant which the defendant is using to harm the claimant. Thus, if a former employee of the claimant has wrongfully taken customer and price lists from the claimant and is using them to compete against the claimant, a search order can be used to recover the stolen lists.

Search orders are also used to obtain evidence of wrongdoing. For example, if a competitor is infringing the claimant's copyright, a search order can be used to search the defendant's premises for evidence of infringing copies, the addresses of suppliers and customers, and details of the profits made by the infringement.

The order has also been used in aid of enforcement (*Distributori Automatica Italia SpA v Holford General Trading Co Ltd and Another* [1985] 1 WLR 1066).

A search order is often made at the same time as a freezing injunction. It can be combined with orders for disclosure and/or further information. It is even possible to obtain an order which prevents the defendant from leaving the country for a short period of time so that he remains available to comply with the search order.

The application must be made in the High Court, the Business List of the Central London County Court or the patents county court. It is always made without notice.

8.3 ENTITLEMENT TO THE ORDER

A search order is a fundamental interference with the defendant's civil liberties. As such, it is only granted in the most extreme cases when the order is needed to ensure that justice is done. The claimant has to prove that he will suffer serious harm and injustice if the order is not made. If the matter can be dealt with in another way, for example by an order for delivery up of goods or preservation of documents under Part 25 of CPR 1998, then it is not an appropriate case for a search order.

In view of the Draconian nature of the order, the comments in Chapter 7 (on freezing injunctions) about the need for detailed inquiries and full disclosure also apply here. The supporting affidavit must disclose very fully the reasons for seeking the order, including the probability that relevant material would disappear if the order was not made. It must also state the address of the premises to be searched and state whether it is a private or business address.

A search order will not be made where there is any doubt about the court's jurisdiction, unless the defendant has been given the opportunity to be heard on the question of jurisdiction (*Altertext Inc v Advanced Data Communications Ltd* [1985] 1 All ER 395). Since such a hearing would defeat the whole point of seeking a search order, it may be preferable in such cases to take proceedings in the defendant's local court. This helps ensure that jurisdiction is not challenged.

8.4 PITFALLS AND SAFEGUARDS

Universal Thermosensors Ltd v Hibben [1992] 3 All ER 257 and *Columbia Picture Industries Inc v Robinson* [1987] Ch 38 are essential reading for solicitors involved in a search order case. They both give detailed guidance on obtaining and executing a search order.

The claimant will have to give the usual undertaking as to damages (see **5.4**), and this will cover oppressive execution of the order, and damages for innocent third parties who have been harmed by the order. The *Columbia Pictures* case shows that aggravated damages can be awarded against a claimant who fails to make proper disclosure or who executes an order oppressively.

It is also very easy for the solicitors involved with a search order to make mistakes. Such mistakes can put them in contempt of court, as in *VDU Installations Ltd v Integrated Computer Systems & Cybernetics* [1989] 1 FSR 378.

The standard form order in PD 25 – Interim Injunctions contains provisions which may help the claimant and his solicitors to avoid such problems.

8.4.1 The supervising solicitor

The standard form order provides that it should be executed by the claimant's solicitor under the guidance of a supervising solicitor who must be experienced in the operation of search orders. The supervising solicitor will be an independent solicitor from some other firm, whose role is to help the defendant understand what is happening and to ensure that nothing unfair happens. The supervising solicitor will have to prepare a report afterwards, which he or she will send to the claimant's solicitor, who will then provide copies for the defendant and the court. The Law Society keeps a list of supervising solicitors (as does the London Solicitors Litigation Association). The claimant's solicitors should file an affidavit, identifying the supervising solicitor's experience in executing search orders.

The order must be served personally by the supervising solicitor.

8.4.2 Dealing with the items the claimant is searching for

The order will specify the items which are the subject of the search (Sch 2 to the order). Only items which are clearly covered by the terms of the order can be removed. *Columbia Pictures* confirms that the claimant cannot take away everything which might be relevant in order to inspect it at his leisure. The applicant's solicitor undertakes to answer forthwith any query made by the defendant as to whether any particular document or article is within the scope of the order.

What happens to the removed items depends on who owns them. If they indisputably belong to the applicant, he can do what he likes with them. Usually, however, the position is not that clear cut.

Often the documents which are taken as evidence belong to the defendant. The applicant's solicitor undertakes to return those originals within 2 working days. During that time, he or she will take copies. Occasionally, the applicant may fear that the defendant will be able to use those documents to cause him further harm. It is possible to modify the undertaking to take account of this but, if the documents are also relevant to the defendant's legitimate activities, he must be allowed some form of access to them.

If ownership of the removed items is disputed, the standard practice (as reflected in the applicant's solicitor's undertakings) is for the applicant's solicitor to retain them until he or she receives an undertaking from the defendant's solicitor to keep the items in safe custody and produce them on request to the court. The applicant's solicitor must then deliver the items to the defendant's solicitor within 2 working days.

The applicant will want to use the items seized as evidence against the defendant in this action. He may also want to use them as evidence of wrongdoing by other people, either by joining them as defendants to the present action or by commencing fresh proceedings against them. This requires the leave of the court (*Crest Homes plc v Marks* [1987] AC 829).

The defendant may also be under investigation by the police, HM Customs & Excise, the Inland Revenue or the Serious Fraud Office. They will be very interested in any information the applicant has about the defendant. The undertaking given by the applicant's solicitor to keep all such items in safe custody, however, means that he or she cannot allow anyone else to see or use the items without the leave of the court. Such leave is rarely granted (*EMI Records Ltd v Spillane* [1986] 1 WLR 967; *General Nutrition v Pradip Pattni* [1984] FSR 403).

Chapter 9

HANDLING THE EVIDENCE

9.1 INTRODUCTION

This chapter builds upon CPR 1998 on disclosure, expert evidence, witness statements and further information (see also the LPC Resource Book *Civil Litigation* (Jordans)). It also looks at the best tactical use of these procedures and how the overriding objective of CPR 1998 and the court's case management powers affect the ways in which evidence is handled in the build up to the trial.

Although this chapter discusses evidence in the context of litigation, the topic is equally important in arbitration and other forms of dispute resolution. Each of the procedures described in this chapter can lead to greater knowledge of the strengths and weaknesses of the client's case. With that knowledge, it is possible to review with the client the likely outcome of the case, the cost of proceeding to the next stage and the appropriate strategy and tactics.

PART I – DISCLOSURE AND INSPECTION

9.2 PRACTICAL POINTS

9.2.1 Practical consequences for the client

Disclosure is a crucial stage in a commercial case. It is often the point at which cases are won or lost because it is the time at which information is exchanged between the parties. Although there are other weapons at the disposal of the parties to obtain information (eg further information or interim applications), disclosure remains central to the action. It is *not* just a matter of listing documents but requires detailed knowledge of the law, in particular regarding which documents are subject to disclosure and/or are privileged. It is an extremely complicated area of the law, which has led to a large amount of case-law over the years. The importance of this stage should not be underestimated, either in terms of its importance to the parties or in the obligations imposed on both sides and their lawyers.

Disclosure is, however, also an expensive stage for the parties in commercial cases. There tend to be a vast number of potentially disclosable documents. It takes time to trace them all and to assess whether they are disclosable and, if so, whether they are privileged. It usually takes just as long to read the opponent's list and to inspect his documents. The solicitor should therefore discuss the costs implications with the client. If the case is weak, it may be better to try and settle before disclosure, rather than waste thousands of pounds in legal costs only to discover what was suspected earlier, ie that the client's cause is a lost one.

9.2.2 Control

Each party must disclose the documents in their control. It is important to realise just how wide this phrase is. It covers not only physical possession or custody of documents but the power to obtain control. Ownership of the document is not required, nor is any legal right or interest in the document. Thus a party must disclose any document which it holds as agent or employee for the true owner, if he issued it in such a capacity. The scope of disclosure in each action must therefore be looked at carefully on its own facts. For example, a director of a company may hold documents in both his personal capacity and also that of shareholder and director. If sued as director, then only the documents which he holds as such would be covered by the disclosure obligations of CPR 1998.

Common areas of difficulty include papers held by a parent company where only the subsidiary is a party to the action and vice versa. Case-law suggests that the test is one of whether the parent company as a matter of fact controls the subsidiary rather than merely owning it. It was held in *Lonrho Ltd v Shell Petroleum Ltd (No 2)* [1980] 1 WLR 627 that documents were not in the control of the parent company, since it had no presently enforceable right to obtain the subsidiary's documents without the latter's consent (the parent could only insist on obtaining them by sacking the board of the subsidiary and replacing it with a new one).

Solicitors are agents of their clients and so may hold disclosable documents to their clients' power (eg title documents to clients' property, correspondence between the clients and third parties). On the other hand, some documents which the solicitor (or other professional agent, eg an accountant) has created for his own purposes (eg attendance notes, working drafts etc) will not be in the control of his client, since they belong to the agent.

Finally, it should be noted that there is no obligation on a party to obtain documents which are not within a party's control, but which he might be able to get hold of. The solicitor should make this point clear to the client and remind him not to obtain any papers from a third party without the solicitor's prior approval, in case by so doing they become disclosable.

9.2.3 Limits

It is important not to lose sight of the fact that one of the purposes of disclosure is to save time and cost. One way of saving costs is to limit the extent of disclosure, particularly in complex cases where there are copious documents. The solicitor should at the outset consider what form of disclosure is best suited to the particular case. If appropriate, he or she should try and agree with the other side a list of the issues in the case and, if possible, a limit on the extent of disclosure. Failing agreement, an application can be made to the court under CPR 1998, r 31.5 for an order which limits the scope of disclosure either generally or, in the first instance, limits disclosure to documents relating to a particular issue (if that issue is likely to be decisive). The party must satisfy the court that further disclosure is either not necessary at all, or not necessary at that stage.

Where appropriate, the parties should also try and agree the method of listing documents (eg to allow generic listing of large numbers of documents of the same type such as invoices). If this is not done, strict compliance with the rules is required and each document should be listed separately.

The better acquainted the solicitor is with all the rules, the better he or she can use them to his or her client's ends and the more pressure that can be brought to bear on the other side during the disclosure process. Successful applications require a good deal of lateral thinking by the solicitor, together with an in-depth knowledge of the nature of the business of both the client and the other party and thus the type of documents which are likely to have been created.

If there are gaps in the list, the matter should first be raised informally with the other side. If this does not work, it is always possible to seek an order for specific disclosure.

As a last resort, if the opponent still fails to make proper disclosure, a solicitor should seek an 'unless order'. If the opponent still fails to comply, his claim or defence can be struck out and the case will be over.

If this is unsuccessful, it will then be for the party who suspects that there has been incomplete disclosure to raise the matter when cross-examining his opponent's witnesses at the trial.

A solicitor should also check for obvious gaps in his or her client's own list before serving it. If the omission will be spotted anyway, it is preferable that the client's own solicitor spots it rather than the opponent.

Disclosure is a continuing obligation. Even after lists have been exchanged, the solicitor must tell the other party if any further relevant documents come into his or her client's possession.

9.8 INADVERTENT DISCLOSURE

If a privileged document is disclosed, this may amount to a waiver of privilege. Similarly, privilege may be waived by allowing inspection of a privileged document. (See *Calcraft v Guest* [1898] 1 QB 759.)

If the error is spotted before inspection takes place, the party at fault should write to the other party explaining the error and explaining why the document is privileged. He will then be entitled to claim privilege and to refuse to allow inspection of the document.

Life becomes more complicated if the other party has been able to see the document. This may arise because of a mistake on inspection but nowadays it is more likely to arise because the privileged documents are delivered to the wrong address by courier or because a fax or e-mail is wrongly addressed.

Under r 31.20:

> 'Where a party inadvertently allows a privileged document to be inspected, the party who has inspected the document may use it or its contents only with the permission of the court.'

The case of *Guinness Peat Properties Ltd v Fitzroy Robinson Partnership* [1987] 2 All ER 716 establishes that an injunction can be granted preventing a party who has received privileged information from making any use of that information if they obtained that information dishonestly or as a result of an obvious mistake.

Example 1

In litigation between A and B, the case has come to trial. The case has been adjourned for lunch. A's barrister has left his or her papers in court during the luncheon adjournment. A clerk in the firm of solicitors acting for B steals A's barrister's papers and copies them during the luncheon adjournment. A can apply for an injunction preventing B from making use of the information contained in the stolen papers. The court will almost certainly grant the injunction.

Example 2

In litigation between A and B, A's solicitors mistakenly send a letter addressed to their client to B's solicitors. A can apply for an injunction to prevent B from making use of the inadvertently disclosed privileged material.

The *Guinness Peat* case generated a significant amount of case-law which established that, where the inadvertent disclosure of privileged material was an obvious mistake, in that a reasonable solicitor would have realised that it was a mistake, the court would grant an injunction restraining the recipient of that information from making any use of it. This culminated in the case of *Ablitt v Mills & Reeve (A Firm) and Another* (1995) *The Times*, October 18.

In that case, the solicitors for the claimant inadvertently delivered several files of privileged documents to the defendant's solicitors. The defendant's solicitors, acting in compliance with the existing *Law Society's Guide to Professional Conduct*, informed their clients of this development. Following the *Law Society's Guide*, they advised their clients that the documents should be returned to the claimant's solicitors unread but that the clients had the right to require their solicitors to read the papers before doing so. They advised their clients of the risk that, if they did read the documents, the court would subsequently grant an injunction preventing the defendant from making any use of the privileged material the solicitors had read, together with orders for costs.

The clients told their solicitors to read the documents. The solicitors did so and then returned the documents to the claimant's solicitors. The claimant applied for an injunction preventing the defendant from making use of the privileged material which had been inadvertently disclosed. The court granted the injunction. It criticised the defendant's solicitors for following the Law Society guidance and asking their clients whether the clients wanted the solicitors to read the documents. The court's injunction effectively disqualified the defendant's solicitors from acting for the defendant in the case in question.

As a result of this case, the Law Society altered its advice to solicitors in such cases. The 8th edition of *The Law Society's Guide to Professional Conduct* (at p 332) simply says that solicitors who receive obviously privileged material as a result of an obvious mistake by their opponent or his lawyers should return the material unread and that 'they may inform' their client of what has happened.

As a result, if a solicitor obviously receives privileged material and it is obvious that this is a result of a mistake, the solicitor should not read the material but should return it unread.

On the other hand, if it is not obvious that the disclosing party has made a mistake, there is no obligation on the receiving party to ask if the disclosure was intended. He

Chapter 11

APPEALS

11.1 INTRODUCTION

The system of appeals in the Civil Justice system in England and Wales was considered by Lord Woolf in his final *Access to Justice* report (HMSO, July 1996) where he defined the purpose of appeals in these terms:

'Appeals serve two purposes: the private purpose, which is to do justice in particular cases by correcting wrong decisions, and the public purpose, which is to ensure public confidence in the administration of justice by making such corrections and to clarify and develop the law and to set precedents.'

Lord Woolf make various recommendations about appeals but in the same year the Lord Chancellor commissioned a full review of civil appellate procedure under Sir Jeffrey Bowman. The 'Bowman Report' was published in September 1997 and was a more detailed version of Lord Woolf's recommendations (Lord Woolf had been a member of the review team).

The review team summarised the purpose of appeals in this way:

'There is a private and public purpose of appeals in civil cases. The private purpose is to correct an error, unfairness or wrong exercise of discretion which has led to an unjust result. The public purpose is to ensure public confidence in the administration of justice and, in appropriate cases, to:

Clarify and develop the law, practice and procedure; and
Help maintain the standards of first instance courts and tribunals.'

The Bowman Report made 146 detailed recommendations, many of which have now been implemented by ss 54–59 of the Access to Justice Act 1999 and Part 52 of CPR 1998, which came into force on 2 May 2000. Guidelines as to the interpretation of the new rules were laid down by the Court of Appeal in *Tanfern Ltd v Cameron-MacDonald and Another* [2001] 1 WLR 1311.

11.2 PART 52

Part 52 of the CPR 1998 and the accompanying practice direction now provide a comprehensive framework of the civil appeals system as it relates to the county court, High Court and Court of Appeal. A crucial aspect of the new system is the requirement for permission to appeal – there is generally no automatic right to appeal. By r 52.3:

'(1) An appellant or respondent requires permission to appeal—

(a)   where the appeal if from a decision of a judge in a county court or the High Court, except where the appeal is against—

(i)   a committal order;

(ii)   a refusal to grant habeas corpus; or

(iii) a secure accommodation order made under section 25 of the Children
      Act 1989(95); or

(b)   as provided by the relevant practice division.

(2) An application for permission to appeal may be made—

(a)   to the lower court at the hearing at which the decision to be appealed was
       made; or
(b)   to the appeal court in an appeal notice.

(Rule 52.4 sets out the time limits for filing an appellant's notice at the appeal
court. Rule 52.5 sets out the time limits for filing a respondent's notice at the
appeal court. Any application for permission to appeal to the appeal court must be
made in the appeal notice (see rules 52.4(1) and 52.5(3).)

(Rule 52.13(1) provides that permission is required from the Court of Appeal for all
appeals to that court from a decision of a county court or the High Court which was
itself made on appeal.)

(3) Where the lower court refuses an application for permission to appeal, a further
application for permission to appeal may be made to the appeal court.

(4) Where the appeal court, without a hearing, refuses permission to appeal, the
person seeking permission may request the decision to be reconsidered at a hearing.

(5) A request under paragraph (4) must be filed within 7 days after service of the
notice that permission has been refused.

(6) Permission to appeal will only be given where—

(a)   the court considers that the appeal would have a real prospect of success; or
(b)   there is some other compelling reason why the appeal should be heard.

(7) An order giving permission may—

(a)   limit the issues to be heard; and
(b)   be made subject to conditions.

(Rule 3.1(3) also provides that the court may make an order subject to conditions.)

(Rule 25.15 provides for the court to order security for costs of an appeal.)'

A request for permission to appeal should therefore generally be made orally to the
court at the conclusion of the hearing at which the decision to be appealed against is
made. If the request is unsuccessful, or no request is made, then the party can apply
for permission from the appeal court itself. A request for permission from the appeal
court should be included in the appeal notice (see **11.5**)

The appeal court will usually deal with a request for permission on paper, without a
hearing. If the request is refused, the appellant can request an oral hearing. If the
request is refused at the oral hearing, that is the end of the matter – there is no further
appeal from this final refusal of permission to appeal by the appeal court.

Permission to appeal will only be given where the court considers that the appeal
would have a real prospect of success or there is some other compelling reason why
the appeal should be heard. In *Tanfern Ltd v Cameron-MacDonald and Another*
[2000] 1 WLR 1311, Brooke LJ stated that 'real prospect of success' has the same
meaning as the test applied in applications for summary judgment. There has to be a
realistic, as opposed to a fanciful, prospect of success.

The other ground for granting permission to appeal – there is some other compelling
reason why the appeal should be heard – could apply, for example, if there is an

arbitrator does not have the power to make orders such as injunctions which carry the sanction of imprisonment for non-compliance. In such cases, the parties and/or the arbitrator can seek the aid of the court under ss 42–44 of AA 1996, so that the court can exercise its wider powers before referring the matter back to the arbitrator.

Another example is that sometimes the parties to a dispute which is being resolved by arbitration will find that the dispute turns on a point of law. Although the arbitrator may decide the point of law for himself, this may lead to an appeal to the court on that point of law (see **12.8**), so it may be preferable to refer the matter to the court under s 45 for a decision on the legal point. Where court involvement is necessary, the matter will normally be dealt with in the Commercial Court.

12.2 THE ARBITRATION AGREEMENT

12.2.1 The terms of the agreement

If the parties to a contract want to ensure that any disputes which may arise are referred to arbitration, they will need to pay considerable attention to the drafting of the arbitration clause. AA 1996 does not provide any assistance here and so it is necessary to rely on prior case-law.

In *Fillite (Runcorn) v Aqualift (A Firm)* (1989) 45 BLR 27, the parties agreed that all 'disputes arising under the contract' should be referred to arbitration. The court held that this clause required the parties only to refer disputes about the duties created by the contract to arbitration, and did not cover allegations of negligent misstatement, misrepresentation or breach of collateral warranties. The court suggested that, for an arbitration clause to cover disputes about those matters, it would have to be phrased to cover disputes 'with reference to the contract'.

Ethiopian Oil Seeds and Pulses Export Corp v Rio del Mar Foods [1990] 1 Lloyd's Rep 86 decided that the words 'arising out of or under the contract' covered all disputes except those about whether the parties had actually formed a contract. Thus, a dispute about the rectification of the contract was covered by the arbitration agreement.

However, in *Ashville Investments Ltd v Elmer Contractors Ltd* [1989] QB 488, the Court of Appeal suggested that the doctrine of precedent should not be rigidly applied in this area of the law. They said that the words of an arbitration clause should always be interpreted in the context of the contract as a whole, bearing in mind the disputes which the parties anticipated at the time. They did, however, hold that a clause referring disputes 'in connection with the contract' to arbitration covered disputes about pre-contract mistake and misrepresentation.

A clause used by the Chartered Institute of Arbitrators for parties who wish to have future disputes referred to arbitration says:

> 'Any dispute arising out of or in connection with this contract shall be referred to and finally resolved by arbitration under the Rules of the Chartered Institute of Arbitrators, which Rules are deemed to be incorporated by reference to this clause.'

This appears comprehensive enough to cover any dispute which could arise, whether it be about the existence, creation, performance or termination of the contract or about related pre-contractual matters.

12.2.2 Incorporating the Arbitration Act 1996

[margin note: S 5]

AA 1996 applies only to arbitration agreements which are in writing (s 5). However, s 5 gives a wide meaning to the term 'agreement in writing'. It covers anything which has been 'recorded by any means' (eg a tape recording) and includes: (i) exchanges of letters or other communications; (ii) agreements evidenced in writing (either by the parties or by a third party acting with the authority of the parties); and (iii) oral agreements to written terms.

By s 5(5), if the parties make written submissions during an arbitration or in court proceedings, and one party alleges that there is a non-written arbitration agreement and the other party does not deny this, those written submissions will create an arbitration agreement to which AA 1996 can apply.

If there is an arbitration agreement, certain provisions of the AA 1996 are mandatory and will apply irrespective of any attempt by the parties to exclude the Act. These provisions are listed in Sch 1 to AA 1996. The relevant mandatory provisions of AA 1996 will be dealt with as and when they are relevant to later parts of this chapter.

A schedule of the main provisions of AA 1996, showing which are mandatory and which are not, appears at the end of this chapter.

As far as the rest of AA 1996 is concerned, the parties can, if they wish, make such arrangements as they see fit. AA 1996 will apply only if the agreement does not cover a particular point which is dealt with in the Act.

12.2.3 Incorporating an arbitration clause

[margin note: S 6(2) could apply to SUB-CONTRACTS]

Even if an agreement does not contain an arbitration clause, it is possible to incorporate an arbitration clause from another document into the agreement by referring to the arbitration clause in such a way as to make it part of the agreement (s 6(2)). For example, in a construction contract, a builder and a land owner might agree in writing to refer all disputes to arbitration. The builder may then enter into a sub-contract with a plumber who will do part of the work required under the main contract. That sub-contract may not itself contain an arbitration clause, but a clause which said 'The provisions of the main contract [the contract between the builder and the land owner] shall apply to this contract unless agreed to the contrary' would be sufficient to incorporate the arbitration clause in the main contract into the sub-contract.

By s 7 of AA 1996, even if the main contract were to be invalid, the arbitration clause would still be effective as far as the sub-contract is concerned.

12.3 APPOINTING THE ARBITRATOR

The arbitration agreement may name the arbitrator. This is rare. It is more usual for the agreement to state how the arbitrator will be appointed.

[margin note: S 15(1)]

Section 15(1) says 'The parties are free to agree on the number of arbitrators to form the tribunal and whether there is to be a chairman or umpire'.

to arbitration in England if there was no risk of being involved in court proceedings in England as well. In such cases, agreements excluding s 45 are likely to be common. Further, it should be noted that, by s 45(1), an agreement that the arbitrator need not give reasons for his decision (see **12.7.3** and **12.8.3**) is deemed to be an agreement to exclude the court's jurisdiction under s 45.

can exclude s45

Different considerations will apply to excluding the court's jurisdiction in 'domestic arbitration agreements' (if these provisions come into force – see **12.1**).

12.5.3 The arbitrator's fee

One additional matter which has to be considered at or before the preliminary meeting (usually when the arbitrator accepts the appointment) is the question of the arbitrator's fee. He will indicate how much he will charge for his services (or the basis on which his fees will be calculated) and how much has to be paid in advance (if any). His agreement to act is conditional on reaching satisfactory agreement about his fee.

12.6 PREPARATIONS FOR THE HEARING

12.6.1 The arbitrator's duties

s33

Both in the preparation for the hearing and during the hearing itself the arbitrator must comply with s 33 of AA 1996. This states that:

'The tribunal shall—

(a) act fairly and impartially as between the parties, giving each party a reasonable opportunity of putting his case and dealing with that of his opponent, and
(b) adopt procedures suitable to the circumstances of the particular case, avoiding unnecessary delay or expense, so as to provide a fair means for the resolution of the matters falling to be determined.'

It goes on to say that:

'The tribunal shall comply with that general duty in conducting the arbitral proceedings, in its decisions on matters of procedure and evidence and in the exercise of all other powers conferred on it.'

At the risk of labouring the obvious, neither the parties nor the arbitrator can contract out of s 33.

Cannot contract out of

12.6.2 The parties' duties

Both in preparing for the hearing and during the hearing itself the parties must comply with s 40 of AA 1996. This states that:

s40

'The parties shall do all things necessary for the proper and expeditious conduct of the arbitral proceedings',

and this includes:

'(a) complying without delay with any determination of the tribunal as to procedural or evidential matters, or with any order or directions of the tribunal, and

Cannot contract out of.

(b)   where appropriate, taking without delay any necessary steps to obtain a decision of the court on a preliminary question of jurisdiction or law'

(see **12.4.3** and **12.5.2**).

Again, the parties cannot contract out of s 40, even with the arbitrator's consent.

12.6.3 Correspondence

Although the preliminary meeting deals with the preparations for the hearing, further problems can arise as time passes by. The arbitrator can call further meetings or he can deal with the problems by correspondence.

Whatever is written to the arbitrator must be copied to the other side. All communications by the arbitrator are sent to both parties.

12.6.4 Want of prosecution

s 41(3)

A party who expects to lose the case may try to postpone the inevitable by failing to co-operate with the arbitrator (eg by failing to reply to correspondence or to attend meetings). If the party in default is the claimant, then the arbitrator can dismiss the claim for want of prosecution under s 41(3) of AA 1996, unless the arbitration agreement states to the contrary (as the parties are free to agree on the arbitrator's powers if a party fails to comply with his s 40 duties (see **12.6.2**)). The arbitrator can do this if there has been inordinate and inexcusable delay which creates a substantial risk that it will not be possible to reach a fair decision or which 'has caused or is likely to cause' the respondent serious prejudice. The arbitrator should not exercise his powers under this section where the limitation period has not expired, unless there are exceptional circumstances (see *James Lazenby & Co v McNicholas Construction Co Ltd* [1995] 1 WLR 615).

12.6.5 Proceeding without notice

If it is the respondent who is not co-operating, the arbitrator may rely on s 41(4) of AA 1996, if either the respondent: (i) is not present at a hearing of which he had been notified; or (ii) fails to provide written evidence or submissions after being given proper notice, and he has not provided a good explanation for his default. This section provides that the arbitrator can deal with the matter on the basis of the arguments and/or evidence provided by the claimant.

12.6.6 Peremptory orders

Under s 41(5) of AA 1996, if any party fails to comply with the arbitrator's directions, the arbitrator can make a peremptory order giving the party in default a specified period of time to comply with the order. If the party does not comply with the order, then, under s 41(7), the arbitrator can either:

s 41(7)

(a)   prevent the party in default from relying on any material which was covered by the order; or
(b)   draw any appropriate adverse inference; or
(c)   proceed to make an award on the basis of the existing evidence; or
(d)   impose costs penalties.

be made only with the permission of the court of first instance (which will usually be the Commercial Court). If the courts continue to follow their previous practices under the earlier legislation, such permission will rarely be granted.

In *Henry Boot Construction (UK) Ltd v Malmaison Hotel (Manchester) Ltd* [2000] 3 WLR 1824, a majority in the Court of Appeal (the matter was obiter) took the view that s 55 of the Access to Justice Act 1999 and CPR 1998, r 52.13 (see Chapter 11) had no effect in relation to an appeal to the Court of Appeal under s 69(8) of AA 1996. Once a party had obtained permission from the court of first instance to appeal, he is not subsequently required to seek permission from the Court of Appeal.

12.9 ENFORCING THE AWARD

Arbitration is the only alternative to litigation which produces a result which can be enforced without commencing litigation.

The normal way of enforcing the award is under s 66 of AA 1996 (which cannot be excluded by the parties). This enables the winning party to apply to the High Court for leave to enforce the award as if it were a court judgment.

s 66

The procedure is set out in the Commercial Court Guide and is beyond the scope of this book.

If leave is granted, the order must be served on the debtor who has 14 days to apply to have it set aside (eg because the award is tainted by misconduct or is wrong in law). (The order must inform the debtor of this right.) If no such application is made or it fails, the applicant can use all the usual methods of enforcement.

12.10 TIME-LIMITS

By s 13 of AA 1996 (which cannot be excluded by the parties), the Limitation Acts apply to arbitrations in the same way as they apply to other disputes. Most arbitration agreements, however, require the parties to commence the arbitration in a much shorter period than the usual limitation period. Once the time-limit in the arbitration agreement has expired, it is normally too late to refer the matter to arbitration, but the arbitration agreement is still effective to prevent either party taking the dispute to the courts, so the aggrieved party will be without a remedy.

s 13

Section 12 of AA 1996 (which cannot be excluded by the agreement of the parties) enables the High Court to grant an extension of time for referring a dispute to arbitration. The parties must first have used any provisions of the arbitration agreement (eg applying to the arbitrator for an extension of time) before applying to the court. The section allows the court only to extend the time for commencing the arbitration.

The grounds for granting an extension are set out in s 12(3). The extension will only be granted in two cases. The first is where 'the circumstances are such as were outside the reasonable contemplation of the parties when they agreed [the time-limit]'. The Court of Appeal considered the correct interpretation of this in *Harbour & General Works Ltd v Environment Agency* [2000] 1 WLR 950. The claimant had narrowly missed the time-limit because of an administrative oversight. The extension was refused on the basis that this was far from so uncommon as to be treated as beyond the parties' contemplation. The Court of Appeal commented that an extension should only be considered where, had the parties known of the circumstances at the time of the agreement, they would at least have contemplated that the time-bar might not apply. The second ground under s 12(3) is that 'the conduct of one party makes it unjust to hold the other party to the strict terms' of the time-limit.

> *Example*
> A and B have an arbitration agreement whereby all disputes must be referred to arbitration within 6 months of the dispute arising. A dispute does arise and A wants to refer the matter to arbitration. B persuades A that this is unnecessary because they will be able to negotiate an amicable settlement. The negotiations appear to be proceeding amicably and a settlement is about to be reached. The day after the 6-month time-limit for referring the dispute to arbitration elapses B withdraws from the negotiations. The implication is that B was not negotiating in good faith and was simply lulling A into a sense of false security, playing for time until the time-limit had expired. This would probably persuade the court to extend the time-limit, provided A does not delay in applying to the court.

Geoffrey Brier QC in *Cathiship SA v Allanasons Ltd, The Catherine Helen* [1998] 3 All ER 714 has ruled that AA 1996 represents a complete change of approach, and that it would now be the exception rather than the rule for the courts to grant extensions of time.

An arbitration agreement may contain other time-limits (eg time-limits for serving documents). It is possible (after exhausting all procedures specified in the arbitration agreement) to apply to the court under s 79 for an order extending such time-limits. The court will extend the time-limit only if 'a substantial injustice would otherwise be done'.

The parties can agree to exclude s 79 in their arbitration agreement. It is likely that such agreements will be common.

12.11 STAYING LITIGATION

Sometimes one of the parties to an arbitration agreement issues court proceedings instead of referring the dispute to arbitration. The defendant must, of course, acknowledge service of the claim form or the claimant will enter a default judgment against him. Having done so, the defendant can then apply to the court under s 9 of AA 1996 for an order staying the court proceedings and referring the matter to arbitration. By Part 11 of CPR 1998, the application must be made within the period for filing a defence. If it is not made in time, the defendant cannot obtain a stay.

By s 9(4), the court will grant a stay unless it is satisfied that 'the arbitration agreement is null and void, inoperative or incapable of being performed'. It will be very rare for these conditions to be satisfied, so the normal course of action will be for the court to grant a stay. In doing so, the fact that the court has powers which the arbitrator does not have (eg to grant summary judgment) is irrelevant. It is also irrelevant that the dispute is about a point of law or, even, that the claimant does not think that there is a dispute and is alleging that the attempt to refer the matter to arbitration by the defendant is simply a ploy to delay payment of compensation.

13.4.2 'Med-arb'

Under this form of ADR, the parties agree to submit their dispute to mediation and that, if this does not work, they will refer the matter to arbitration. They may, if they wish, use the person who has been acting as their mediator as their arbitrator. This will save costs because the arbitrator will already know the facts of the case. There is a risk, however, that, during the mediation, he will have become privy to confidential information belonging to one of the parties. This would compromise his position as arbitrator, so any agreement for 'med-arb' should give either party the right to object to the mediator becoming the arbitrator.

13.4.3 'Mini-trial' or 'structured settlement procedure'

Under this procedure, the parties appoint a neutral who will sit as chairman of a tribunal composed of himself and a senior representative of each of the parties. These representatives may not be immediately connected with the dispute and should have authority to reach such compromise as they see fit. They will then hear and/or read the cases of the two parties (sometimes with an expert), after which they will negotiate with each other with the help of the independent arbiter.

13.4.4 Expert appraisal and Early Neutral Evaluation

In expert appraisal, the parties refer all or part of their dispute to an expert in the disputed field or to a lawyer for his opinion. His opinion is not binding on the parties, but it is hoped that it will help them to reach a settlement. If that is not possible, the process may nevertheless be useful in focusing the parties' attention on the evidence they require to put their case effectively. It is for the parties and their expert to choose the appropriate procedure which could involve a short trial and/or written submissions before the expert makes his recommendation.

The Commercial Court offers a similar procedure, the early neutral evaluation scheme under which litigants can ask for a preliminary view on the merits from a Commercial Court judge. It is usually agreed that, if a settlement is not reached, the judge will have no further involvement in the action.

13.4.5 Judicial appraisal

CEDR has a scheme whereby former judges and senior counsel are available to give a quick preliminary view on the legal position, having heard representations from both parties. It is a matter for agreement between the parties as to whether this opinion is to be binding on them or not.

13.4.6 Expert determination

Expert determination is a halfway house between arbitration and ADR. As in arbitration, the parties select an expert to decide the case for them. They agree to accept his decision and, if one fails to do so, the other can sue for breach of contract. The expert's decision cannot, however, be enforced as a court order and he does not have the powers of an arbitrator under AA 1996. Also, unlike an arbitrator, he can be sued in negligence by a party who thinks his decision was wrong, although the expert may be hard to challenge because he is not usually obliged to give reasons for his decision. At present, expert determination is most commonly used for rent reviews

Rent reviews & Accountancy valuations [handwritten margin note]

and accountancy valuations. Whilst it is simple, quick and relatively cheap, the client is unlikely to be able to challenge the outcome if he does not like the decision. Careful thought should, therefore, be given to whether this method is suitable for resolving a particular dispute (see also **12.14**).

13.4.7 Final offer arbitration

The parties can instruct their chosen neutral that they will both make an offer of the terms on which they will settle and that he must choose one of those two offers and no other solution. Neither party can afford to make an unrealistic offer because that will mean that the neutral will choose the opponent's offer, so, at least in theory, the offers are likely to be realistic.

13.4.8 Adjudication

This is a statutory procedure under the Housing Grants, Construction and Regeneration Act 1996 available to resolve commercial construction disputes and intended to be quicker and cheaper than arbitration. The process is most often used by parties involved in long-term projects. The adjudicator determines disputes that arise in the course of the project so that it is not delayed by a lengthy disagreement and/or litigation. The parties may retain the right to litigate the dispute on completion of the project if they so choose. Subject to this, the adjudicator's decision is binding. However, it can be enforced only by issuing proceedings and applying for a summary judgment (*Macob Civil Engineering Ltd v Morrison Construction Ltd* [1999] 3 EGLR 7, QBD).

13.5 ORGANISATIONS PROVIDING ADR

At present, anyone can provide help in resolving disputes, but the job is not as easy as it sounds. It should be done by someone who has been trained. The two main organisations who have pioneered ADR in commercial matters, in this country, are CEDR and the ADR Group.

CEDR's address is Princes House, 95 Gresham Street, London EC2V 7NA. It is an independent, non-profit making organisation promoting ADR, which runs training courses and maintains a panel of neutrals.

ADR Group is based at Grove House, Grove Road, Redland, Bristol BS6 6UN. It is a private company which undertakes mediation and training and has established a network of mediators in firms of solicitors throughout the country.

Two other organisations which are very active in the field of ADR, although their principal raison d'être arose from other functions, are the Chartered Institute of Arbitrators (International Arbitration Centre, 24 Angel Gate, City Road, London EC3R 6DS) and the Academy of Experts (2 South Square, Gray's Inn, London WC1R 5HP).

Finally, there is Mediation UK, whose general services include all forms of mediation. Their address is Alexander House, Telephone Avenue, Bristol BS1 4BS.

Many professional bodies, like the Royal Institution of Chartered Surveyors, provide ADR services for disputes involving their members.

As mentioned at **13.4.4**, the judges of the Commercial Court may be prepared to offer their services to help litigants to resolve their disputes without going to trial.

13.6 USING ADR

Parties to a dispute can always reach an ad hoc agreement, when the dispute arises, to use any form of ADR they see fit to solve their problems. It is more pro-active, however, to agree in the original contract that, if any dispute does arise between the parties, they will resolve it by some specified form of ADR.

Such contracts are usually not binding (but see **13.3.1**), because any party can always choose litigation instead (compare arbitration agreements), but they do give the parties an opportunity to resolve their disputes peaceably. There is a strong case for recommending that existing contracts which include an arbitration agreement should be amended, so that the agreement provides for mediation before the parties go to formal arbitration (which they would do only if mediation failed).

13.6.1 Disclosure obligations

An agreement to use ADR should include clauses dealing with some of the potential pitfalls associated with ADR. The parties should decide whether to have a clause requiring full disclosure. The drawback of such a clause is that, the more information the parties have to provide for each other, the longer the process may take and the more costly it will be. Its advantage is that it would be possible to set aside a settlement reached, as a result of ADR, on discovering that one of the parties had concealed vital information. To prevent vexatious applications to set aside any settlement, it might be wise to stipulate in the disclosure clause that a settlement can only be challenged for fundamental non-disclosure of matters which would significantly have affected the result of the ADR process.

13.6.2 Confidentiality

A confidentiality clause in the agreement will encourage full disclosure. The mediator is always under a duty of confidentiality, but the parties will be more likely to disclose information to each other if they know that the other party has agreed not to divulge the information to anyone else. However, if the parties are commercial rivals, who need to keep information secret from each other, disclosure and confidentiality clauses are pointless.

13.6.3 Other matters

An ADR agreement should explain how the arbiter will be appointed and specify the procedure he should follow. It should also specify that the representatives who attend any ADR process must have full authority to settle the dispute there and then.

13.7 CHOOSING ADR

A solicitor should discuss with the client the possible uses of ADR whenever a dispute arises in a commercial matter. If the client is willing (or has already agreed) to use ADR, it should be used unless it is obviously inappropriate, for example, because an injunction is required or the other party cannot be trusted to comply with an award or to co-operate in the process. There is no point, however, in proceeding with ADR if it looks like failing. In such cases, at the first sign of non-co-operation or lack of trust (eg where the opponent will not help in the selection of the neutral), litigation or arbitration should be used. This does not necessarily mean abandoning ADR. It may be appropriate to continue with ADR in conjunction with litigation, using the latter as a spur to co-operation with the former.

13.8 THE FUTURE OF ADR

Although ADR is still used in a minority of commercial cases, it is becoming increasingly popular. An important factor has been the introduction of CPR 1998, which emphasise that litigation should be a last resort. The potential penalties attached to claimants' Part 36 offers have made defendants, particularly insurers, far more eager to explore settlement at an early stage. In addition, where litigation is being conducted under a conditional fee agreement, this may have the effect of encouraging the solicitor to promote settlement initiatives, including ADR: a quick settlement which generates a success fee is an attractive option when the alternative could be lengthy litigation without remuneration.

The Lord Chancellor's Department has been considering, and consulting on, issues relevant to ADR. These include whether providers should be regulated and how greater use of ADR can be encouraged by the courts. One possibility is that in a civil or commercial dispute, litigants could be obliged to try ADR and could face penalties (most probably in costs) for refusing to do so or for a lack of good faith during negotiations. However, forcing the parties to the negotiating table may be counterproductive, particularly during the early stages of a dispute when feelings often run high. Also, assessing whether a party has acted with a lack of good faith may be difficult unless the parties or the mediator are required to divulge privileged or confidential information. It is also possible that obliging parties to engage in ADR could be challenged as a contravention of the right to a fair trial under Article 6(1) of the European Convention on Human Rights.

13.9 SUMMARY

ADR involves an independent third party who helps the parties to resolve their dispute. The parties are usually free to dispense with his services whenever they see fit. It can provide a quick and cheap means of resolving a dispute in a commercially sensible manner, although the result may not be entirely in accordance with the parties' legal rights and cannot be enforced in the same way as a court judgment or an arbitrator's award.

Solicitors advising commercial clients should be aware of the wide range of ADR techniques and of the organisations who offer help with these techniques. It may be helpful to include ADR agreements in commercial contracts, but careful thought needs to be given to the details of such agreements on matters like disclosure and confidentiality.

13.10 FURTHER READING

Brown and Marriott *ADR Principles and Practice* 2nd edn (Sweet & Maxwell, 1999).

Mackie, Miles and Marsh *Commercial Dispute Resolution: An ADR Practice Guide* 2nd edn (Butterworths, 2000).

(eg a bank, building society or finance house) the judgment creditor should serve the garnishee at its head office. It is also good practice to serve a copy on the branch where the judgment debtor has his account. The judgment creditor will then serve the order on the judgment debtor.

There will then be an on notice hearing at which the court will decide whether to order the garnishee to pay the money to the judgment creditor. At that hearing (called the hearing of the 'garnishee order absolute') the court will also consider whether the order would prejudice other creditors of the judgment debtor. If the garnishee does not appear or does not dispute the debt, the court will usually make the garnishee order absolute, ie a final order which will be enforced against the garnishee. If the garnishee denies the debt, the court will have to investigate his claim before deciding whether to order him to pay the judgment creditor or to refuse to make the order absolute.

The court cannot garnishee a joint bank account or other jointly owned debt if the other owners do not owe the judgment creditor money.

Charging orders on land (RSC Ord 50, CCR Ord 31)

A charging order gives the judgment creditor a charge over the judgment debtor's land. If the land is jointly owned then (if the co-owner is not a party to the debt) only the judgment debtor's beneficial interest in the land can be charged.

The judgment creditor applies without notice for a charging order nisi, giving full details of any other creditors known to him. The charging order nisi temporarily charges the judgment debtor's land and fixes a hearing date when the judgment creditor will apply for the order to be made final or absolute. The judgment creditor then serves the order on the judgment debtor. The court may also direct him to serve the order on one or more of the judgment debtor's other creditors and any other interested person (eg the judgment debtor's spouse or any other person living in the property). These people will be able to argue at the hearing that the order should not be made absolute.

In the meantime, the judgment creditor will register the order nisi at HM Land Registry or the Land Charges Registry, as appropriate, to prevent any dealings with the land pending the hearing. Where the land is registered land, the order is protected by a notice or caution at HM Land Registry. In the case of unregistered land, the order is registered at the Land Charges Registry as a writ or order affecting land. If the land is jointly owned land and one of the owners is not a debtor, then a caution may be lodged if it is registered land. However, where the land is unregistered land, it may not be protected by registering a Land Charge (see Sch 3, para 12 to the Trusts of Land and Appointment of Trustees Act 1996, which inserts s 6(1A) of the Land Charges Act 1972). There may be little point in practice, therefore, in obtaining a charging order over a debtor's beneficial interest in jointly owned unregistered land, when it cannot be protected by registration.

The judgment creditor should also give notice of the order to anyone else who has a charge over the land.

The court has a discretion whether to make the charging order absolute, although the burden of proof is on the judgment debtor and the others opposing the order. It will not make the order absolute if there is a reasonable chance that the debt will be paid in the near future or if the debt is relatively small compared to the value of the property to be charged. Nor will it make the order if it would give the applicant an unfair advantage over the other creditors. If the judgment debtor has been made bankrupt or wound up, the order will normally be refused (*Roberts Petroleum Ltd v Bernard Kenny Ltd* [1983] 2 AC 192). If the court does not make the order absolute, it will discharge the order.

Sometimes the judgment debtor will be involved in divorce proceedings when the judgment creditor applies for the charging order. If the judgment debtor's spouse is seeking a transfer of property order under s 24 of the Matrimonial Causes Act 1973, the application for a charging order should be transferred to the Family Division, so that that court can deal with both matters at the same time. Even so, that court is unlikely to transfer the property to the judgment debtor's spouse if this would defeat the claims of the creditors. The most the court is likely to do is to protect the spouse's right to occupy the house by placing restrictions on the circumstances in which it can be sold (*First National Securities Ltd v Hegerty* [1984] 3 WLR 769; *Harman v Glencross* [1986] 2 WLR 637).

If the court makes the order absolute, the judgment creditor will register it in the same way as he registered the order nisi. This ensures that when the judgment debtor sells the land, the judgment creditor is paid from the proceeds of sale. In the meantime the charge merely provides the judgment creditor with security. However, it may be some time before the judgment debtor decides to sell the land and the judgment creditor is paid from the proceeds of sale. If, therefore, the judgment creditor wishes to force the judgment debtor to sell the land, to realise the monies, he may apply for an order for sale. This is done by commencing new proceedings (RSC Ord 88, r 5A). It is in the court's discretion whether it makes an order for sale and it is unlikely to do so if the amount of the debt secured by the charge is small.

Attachment of earnings (CCR Ord 27)

Where the judgment debtor is employed and the judgment creditor is willing to accept payment by instalments, an attachment of earnings order in the county court may be an appropriate method of enforcement. The order directs the judgment debtor's employer to deduct instalments, usually on a weekly or monthly basis, from the judgment debtor's earnings in repayment of the judgment debt. This method of enforcement is usually inappropriate in commercial cases.

14.4.3 Other methods of enforcement

(1) Land (RSC Ord 45, r 3; CCR Ord 26, r 17)

A writ of possession (or warrant of possession in the county court) is the usual method of enforcing a judgment for possession of land (eg following forfeiture proceedings, etc), although committal and sequestration (see **6.5.4** and **6.5.5**) can also be used.

(2) Enforcement of judgment for the delivery of goods (RSC Ord 45, r 4; CCR Ord 26, r 16)

A claimant may obtain judgment for delivery up of goods, for example where he successfully sues for wrongful interference with goods under the Torts (Interference with Goods) Act 1977. Another example of such a judgment is where the claimant is granted specific performance following a breach of contract claim, under the Sale of Goods Act 1979. Usually there are two types of judgment, one which allows the

PART II

FOREIGN ELEMENT

Chapter 15

FOREIGN ELEMENT: COMMENCING PROCEEDINGS

15.1 INTRODUCTION

When first instructed in relation to a potential piece of litigation, the solicitor will have to consider, as one of the preliminary steps, where the action should be conducted or, if an action has already commenced, whether proceedings have been issued in the correct country. These preliminary considerations are essential, particularly where one of the parties, or the subject matter of the action, is foreign or located abroad.

There are different complex sets of rules which apply to determine jurisdiction and which depend on whether the foreign country involved (whether because of the nationality/domicile of one of the parties or the subject matter of the action) is an EU State, part of the UK or somewhere else in the world.

In a contractual dispute, it is essential for the solicitor to check whether the contract contains an arbitration or jurisdiction clause which takes precedence over the applicable rules (see **15.2.2** and **15.2.10**).

The Brussels Convention on Jurisdiction and the Enforcement of Judgments in Civil and Commercial Matters 1968 (the Brussels Convention) dealt with the issue of jurisdiction as between Member States of the European Community (EC). In a slightly amended form, it became part of English law by virtue of the Civil Jurisdiction and Judgments Act 1982 (CJJA 1982). CJJA 1982 also regulates jurisdiction as between the various parts of the UK.

The Lugano Convention on Jurisdiction and the Enforcement of Judgments in Civil and Commercial Matters 1988 (the Lugano Convention) effectively extended the rules in the Brussels Convention to the Member States of the European Free Trade Association (EFTA). It became part of English law by virtue of the Civil Jurisdiction and Judgments Act 1991.

The Channel Islands and the Isle of Man are not part of the UK or the EU. They are subject to the common law rules on jurisdiction which the English courts apply to the rest of the world.

This chapter deals first with the rules in the Brussels Convention which decide which State's courts have jurisdiction in litigation involving parties based in different Member States of the European Union. The CJJA 1982, however, also had to deal with the fact that, although the UK is a Member State of the European Union, it has three internal jurisdictions (England and Wales, Scotland, and Northern Ireland). CJJA 1982 had to deal with the problem of litigants based in different jurisdictions within the UK. In the main, it adopted the rules of the Brussels Convention, but it did depart from this Convention in four cases, which are dealt with at **15.3**.

In reading this chapter, it will become apparent that there are some cases where a party will be able to commence proceedings in more than one State, and **15.7–15.9**

The defendant can also object to proceedings in one part of the UK on the grounds that proceedings have already been commenced in another part of the UK (see **15.6.1**).

15.6.3 One of the parties is based outside the EU

If one of the parties is based outside the EU, that party can object to the jurisdiction of the English courts on the ground that the English courts are not the most appropriate ones for resolving the dispute. He has to prove that it is possible for the claimant to issue proceedings in another State. The claimant then has to prove that the English courts are the most convenient place to deal with the litigation bearing in mind the convenience of the parties and the witnesses and the interests of justice (*Spiliada Maritime Corp v Cansulex, The Spiliada* [1987] AC 460).

The technical term for this objection is forum non conveniens. In multi-party litigation, if part of the proceedings have been commenced outside the EU that party can raise the issue of forum non conveniens even though all the other parties are based in the EU (*Re Harrods (Buenos Aires) Ltd* [1992] Ch 72).

In *Connelly v RTZ Corporation* [1997] 3 WLR 373, the claimant commenced proceedings in England against defendants based in Namibia. The defendants objected to the jurisdiction on the grounds that the incident occurred in Namibia and all the witnesses lived in Namibia. The claimant argued that he could not afford to bring proceedings in Namibia because he would not qualify for legal aid there and that the only way in which he could afford to bring proceedings anywhere in the world was to bring them in England where he could get legal aid. The House of Lords decided that the English courts were the most convenient place to deal with the case (presumably on the basis that it was more convenient to have an inconvenient trial than no trial at all).

15.6.4 Interim relief

Even if proceedings are stayed, it is still possible for the English courts to grant one of the parties an interim injunction (*Phonogram Ltd v DEF American Inc* (1994) *The Times*, October 7).

15.7 WHERE TO SUE (OR BE SUED)

An English client will usually prefer to resolve his disputes in England and his solicitor must study the jurisdiction rules carefully to achieve this result wherever appropriate. There are, however, three potential drawbacks to English proceedings against a foreign defendant.

(1) If the contract is governed by foreign law, the parties will have to call expert evidence regarding the law in question. This can be very expensive.
(2) If the defendant's property is outside the jurisdiction, there can be a delay in enforcing judgment (see Chapter 16).
(3) If the harm caused by the defendant's tort has occurred in more than one State within the EU, it may be preferable to sue in the defendant's 'home State' (see **15.2.6**).

Canada.

(4) Where the dispute concerns a contract, it is also possible (under the principle in *Leathertex Divisione Sintetici SpA v Bodetex BVBA* – see **15.2.5**) that only the defendant's home court will be able to deal with the entire dispute.

15.8 THE PERILS OF FOREIGN LITIGATION

There will be cases where it is not possible to avoid litigation in a foreign country or where it is desirable to take proceedings abroad. A solicitor will instruct foreign lawyers as agents, but he or she will still have to bear certain dangers in mind.

15.8.1 Limitation periods

Foreign limitation periods may be much shorter than the English equivalents.

15.8.2 Causes of action

Some countries may not recognise a cause of action which is part of English law. Others may allow claims which would not be actionable here.

15.8.3 Remedies

Remedies may differ, especially at the interim stage. For example, not all countries have an equivalent to our search orders, while other countries exercise much tighter control over the defendant's property pending trial than we do under the freezing injunction and give creditors greater rights to an early judgment.

15.8.4 Time

The time it takes for an action to come to trial can vary widely from State to State. There is a significant difference between, for example, the pace of German and Italian litigation.

15.8.5 Costs

In most countries, costs follow the event but this is not always the case and, even where costs are awarded to the winner, they may be based on the value of the claim rather than the amount of work involved. Contingency fee systems are common.

15.8.6 Judicial expertise

In some countries, the judges will have considerable commercial expertise, being local businessmen themselves. Alternatively, the judges may be aided by lay assessors.

15.8.7 Miscellaneous

There may also be different rules on, for example, whether a claim carries interest or on the enforcement of judgments.

15.9 COMMON LAW VERSUS CIVIL LAW

Common law systems like those used in the USA and most Commonwealth countries will have many features with which an English lawyer will be familiar, although there may well be differences in, for example, contingency fees, the level of costs and the amount of pre-trial disclosure.

Civil law systems are very different. For a start, there will be no (or very limited) disclosure of documents. The main difference, however, lies in the role of the judge. We are used to the case building to a formal climax (the trial) at which the parties have a major say in what evidence the judge is to hear. That is not what happens in most of the rest of Europe.

Under the civil code systems, if the parties choose to litigate then, generally, they place themselves in the hands of a judge who has to decide where the truth lies. The judge investigates the case. He interviews the parties. He then decides what witnesses he would like to hear and questions those witnesses. In some countries, the parties' lawyers are then entitled to ask their own questions of the witness. In other countries, the lawyers are not allowed to speak to the witnesses at all.

The judge also decides whether expert evidence is needed and, if it is, he usually chooses who that expert will be. It can be extremely difficult to challenge the views of such an expert.

As a result, litigation elsewhere in Europe places much greater emphasis on detailed statements of case and written evidence than an English lawyer is accustomed to. On the other hand, the rules on admissibility of evidence tend to be less complex and cross-examination of witnesses is relatively rare.

The CPR 1998 have reduced, to some extent, the differences between English and European litigation as English judges take more and more responsibility for managing the case, appointing experts, and deciding what evidence they wish to hear.

15.10 SUMMARY

The law relating to jurisdiction is not the easiest piece of law to come to grips with. It is important to remember that there are two entirely different systems.

The first system applies where all parties are based in different States of the EU or different parts of the UK. Such cases are governed by the Brussels and Lugano Conventions and the Civil Jurisdiction and Judgments Acts 1982 and 1991.

① Parties in EU

The basic rule is that the claimant must issue proceedings in the defendant's local courts. There are exceptions to this rule, of which the most important are those which apply in contract cases or tort cases, cases where one court has exclusive jurisdiction (especially cases relating to land), and cases where the parties have entered into a jurisdiction agreement.

The rules where both parties are based in different States of the EU and where both parties are based in different parts of the UK are largely the same, although there are four differences, which are set out at **15.3**.

16.5.3 Enforcement abroad

To enforce a judgment abroad, the evidence in support of the application for a certified copy of the judgment merely has to give details of the judgment, the territory where the debtor resides, and the names, trades and addresses of both parties. Apart from that, the procedure is broadly the same as under CJJA 1982.

16.6 COMMON LAW

If the judgment is one to which the above procedures do not apply (either because of the nature of the judgment or because it was made in a State which is not covered by them), its enforcement here is a matter for the common law.

16.6.1 Recognition

The judgment will not be recognised at common law if:

(1) the proceedings were contrary to natural justice (eg the defendant was not given a fair chance to be heard);
(2) it was obtained by fraud;
(3) recognition would be contrary to public policy;
(4) the foreign court lacked jurisdiction;
(5) the judgment is covered by s 5 of the Protection of Trading Interests Act 1980 (which is primarily aimed at US anti-trust legislation).

16.6.2 Enforcement here

It is always open to a foreign judgment creditor to commence fresh proceedings in England if he has a cause of action here. More usually, however, he will treat the foreign judgment as a contract containing an implied promise to pay the judgment debt. He will issue proceedings alleging breach of that contract and apply for summary judgment under Part 24 of CPR 1998. (The court can award interest on the judgment.) This method is only available to him if the foreign judgment is a final judgment for the payment of a fixed sum of money. If there is an appeal in the foreign court, proceedings in this country to enforce the judgment may be stayed.

16.6.3 Enforcement there

Enforcement abroad is a matter for the law and courts of the country where the creditor is seeking to enforce an English judgment.

16.7 SUMMARY

The procedure for enforcing an English judgment in a foreign country or a foreign judgment in England depends on the place where enforcement is to take place. If the creditor wishes to enforce the judgment in another EU State or another part of the UK, he must comply with the rules laid down under the Civil Jurisdiction and Judgments Acts 1982 and 1991 (see **16.2** and, if the judgment is to be enforced elsewhere in the UK, **16.3**). If the creditor wishes to enforce the judgment in a Commonwealth or former Commonwealth State, he will probably have to use the procedures laid down under either the FJ(RE)A 1933 or the AJA 1920 (see **16.4** and **16.5**). If there is no Act of Parliament governing enforcement in the foreign State, the common law or the law of the State where the judgment is to be enforced will apply (see **16.6**).

16.8 FURTHER READING

Kaye *Civil Jurisdiction and Enforcement of Foreign Judgments* (Professional Books, 1987).

Appendix B

CASE MANAGEMENT INFORMATION SHEET

Party lodging information sheet

Name of solicitors

Name(s) of advocates for trial

[Notes: This sheet should normally be completed with the involvement of the advocate(s) instructed for trial. If the claimant is a litigant in person this fact should be noted at the foot of the sheet and proposals made as to which party is to have responsibility for the preparation and upkeep of the case management bundle.]

(1)   By what date can you give standard disclosure?

(2)   In relation to standard disclosure, do you contend in relation to any category or class of document under CPR 1998, r 31.6(b) that to search for that category or class would be unreasonable? If so, what is the category or class and on what grounds do you so contend?

(3)   Is specific disclosure required on any issue (specifying which)?

(4)   Is a special disclosure order appropriate?

(5)   By what dates can you (a) give specific disclosure or (b) comply with a special disclosure order?

(6)   May the time periods for inspection at CPR 1998, r 31.15 require adjustment, and if so by how much?

(7)   Are amendments to or is information about any statement of case required? If yes, please give brief details of what is required.

(8)   Can you make any additional admissions? If yes, please give brief details of the additional admissions.

(9)   Are any of the issues in the case suitable for trial as preliminary issues?

(10)   a.   On the evidence of how many witnesses of fact do you intend to rely at trial (subject to the directions of the court)? Please give their names, or explain why this is not being done.
        b.   By what date can you serve signed witness statements?
        c.   How many of these witnesses of fact do you intend to call to give oral evidence at trial (subject to the directions of the court)? Please give their names, or explain why this is not being done.
        d.   Will interpreters be required for any witness?
        e.   Do you wish any witness to give oral evidence by video link? Please give his or her name, or explain why this is not being done. Please state the country and city from which the witness will be asked to give evidence by video link.

(11)   a.   On what issues may expert evidence be required?

Appendix F

LIST OF DOCUMENTS: STANDARD DISCLOSURE

List of documents: standard disclosure

Notes:

* The rules relating to standard disclosure are contained in Part 31 of the Civil Procedure Rules and Section E of the Commercial Court Guide.

* Documents to be included under standard disclosure are contained in Rule 31.6

* A document has or will have been in your control if you have or have had possession, or a right of possession, of it **or** a right to inspect or take copies of it.

In the	High Court of Justice Queen's Bench Division Commercial Court Royal Courts of Justice
Claim No.	
Claimant(s) (including ref)	
Defendant(s) (including ref)	
Date	
Party returning this form	

Disclosure Statement of (Claimant)(Defendant)

1. (I/We), (name(s)) state that (I/we) have carried out a reasonable search to locate all the documents which (I am or .... *here name the party* is) required to disclose under (the order made by the court *or* the agreement in writing made between the parties on) *(insert date)*

2. The extent of the search that (I/we) made to locate documents that (I am *or here name the party* is) required to disclose was as follows:

3. (I/We) limited the search in the following respects:-
   a. (I/We) did not search for documents
   1. pre-dating

   2. located in the following places

   3. in the following categories or classes

   b.*(Other limits, if any, e.g. documents post-dating*

N265(CC) -w3- standard disclosure (4.99)   *Produced on behalf of The Court Service*

4. The facts considered in arriving at the decision that it was reasonable to limit the search in the respects identified above were as follows *(the facts must be set out in detail: see paragraph E3.6 of the Commercial Court Guide):*

```



```

5. (I/We) certify that (I/we) understand the duty of disclosure and to the best of (my/our) knowledge (I have *or here name the party* has) carried out that duty. (I/We) further certify that the list above is a complete list of all documents which are or have been in (my *or here name the party's*) control which (I am *or here name the party* is) obliged under (the said order *or* the said agreement in writing) to disclose.

6. (I *or here name the party*) understand(s) that (I *or here name the party*) must inform the court and the other parties immediately if any further documents required to be disclosed by Rule 31.6 comes into (my *or here name the party's*) control at any time before the conclusion of the case.

7. ((I *or here name the party*) (have/has) not permitted inspection of documents within the category or class of documents (as set out below) required to be disclosed under Rule 31(6)(b) or (c) on the grounds that to do so would be disproportionate to the issues in the case.)

```



```

Signed |_____| **Date** |_____|

Name(s) |_____|

Position or office held |_____|

Please state why you are the appropriate person(s) to make the disclosure statement.

```



```

Appendix I

SUMMARY OF ALTERNATIVE PROCEDURE FOR CLAIMS UNDER PART 8

The Part 8 procedure is usually used in cases where there is no substantial dispute of fact, for example in cases where the only issue is the construction of a document or a statute.

1. Claimant issues Part 8 claim form and serves the claim form and supporting written evidence*

NB: there are no particulars of claim.

2. Defendant acknowledges service and files written evidence in support*

Within 14 days of service of the claim form.

The defendant must notify the court if he does not intend to file any evidence.

NB: there is no defence and no possibility of the claimant entering judgment in default.

3. Claimant's written evidence in reply[1]

Within 14 days of receipt of defendant's written evidence (if any evidence in reply is required).

The parties may extend this time-limit to a maximum of 28 days by written agreement. The agreement must be filed at court. Any longer extension requires an application to the court.

NB: no allocation questionnaires are filed.

4. The court gives directions or fixes a hearing date

The court may have given case management directions when the claim was issued, but will often consider its file for the purpose of deciding how the case should be dealt with after the expiry of the defendant's deadline for filing evidence.

If necessary the court can hold a case management conference, but in many cases no oral directions hearing is required. Instead, the court may be able to make a **final order in writing** or to **direct a hearing before a judge** (to resolve the substantive issues). The Judge can require oral evidence to be given, but will more commonly rely on the parties' written evidence.

---

[1] The evidence is in the form of witness statement(s) or affidavit(s).

(2) If the Respondent wishes to defend the Claim where the Claim Form states that Particulars of Claim are to follow, he must complete and return the Acknowledgement of Service within [ ] days of being served with the Claim Form. Where the Particulars of Claim are served with the Claim Form, and the Respondent wishes to defend part or all of the Claim he must complete and return an Acknowledgement of Service within [ ] days of being served with the Claim Form or a Defence within [ ] days.

GUIDANCE NOTES

EFFECT OF THIS ORDER

(1) A Respondent who is an individual who is ordered not to do something must not do it himself or in any other way. He must not do it through others acting on his behalf or on his instructions or with his encouragement.

(2) A Respondent which is a corporation and which is ordered not to do something must not do it itself or by its directors, officers, employees or agents or in any other way.

VARIATION OR DISCHARGE OF THIS ORDER

The Respondent (or anyone notified of this Order) may apply to the Court at any time to vary or discharge this Order (or do much of it as affects that person), but anyone wishing to do so must first inform the Applicant's Legal Representatives.

PARTIES OTHER THAN THE APPLICANT AND RESPONDENT

(1) Effect of this Order: It is a Contempt of Court for any person notified of this Order knowingly to assist in or permit a breach of this Order. Any person doing so may be sent to prison, fined or have his assets seized.

(2) Set off by banks: This injunction does not prevent any bank from exercising any right of set off it may have in respect of any facility which it gave to the Respondent before it was notified of this Order.

(3) Withdrawals by the Respondent: No bank need enquire as to the application or proposed application of any money withdrawn by the Respondent if the withdrawal appears to be permitted by this Order.

INTERPRETATION OF THIS ORDER

(1) In this Order, where there is more than one Respondent, (unless otherwise stated), references to 'the Respondent' means both or all of them.

(2) A requirement to serve on 'the Respondent' means on each of them. However, the Order is effective against any Respondent on whom it is served.

(3) An order requiring 'the Respondent' to do or not to do anything applies to all Respondents.

<u>COMMUNICATIONS WITH THE COURT</u>

All communications to the Court about this Order should be sent, where the Order is made in the Chancery Division, to Room TM 510, Royal Courts of Justice, Strand, London WC2A 2LL quoting the case number. The telephone number is 020 7936 6827. Where the order is made in the Queen's Bench Division, communications should be sent to Room W11 (020 7936 6009). The offices are open between 10 am and 4.30 pm Monday to Friday.

SCHEDULE A

AFFIDAVITS

The Applicant relied on the following affidavits:

[*name*]	[*number of affidavits*]	[*date sworn*]	[*filed on behalf of*]

(1)

(2)

SCHEDULE B

UNDERTAKINGS GIVEN TO THE COURT BY THE APPLICANT

(See **7.5** above)

NAME AND ADDRESS OF APPLICANT'S LEGAL REPRESENTATIVES

The Applicant's Legal Representatives are:

[Name, address, reference, fax and telephone numbers both in and out of office hours.]

Appendix O

NOTICE OF APPEAL

Appellant's Notice

In the

Notes for guidance are available which will help you complete this form. Please read them carefully before you complete each section.

Seal

For Court use only	
Appeal Court Reference No.	
Date filed	

Section 1	Details of the claim or case

Name of court _____

Case or claim number _____

Names of claimants/ applicants/ petitioner

Names of defendants/ respondents

In the case or claim, were you the
(tick appropriate box)

☐ claimant   ☐ applicant   ☐ petitioner

☐ defendant   ☐ respondent   ☐ other *(please specify)* _____

Section 2	Your (appellant's) name and address

Your (appellant's) name _____

Your solicitor's name _____ *(if you are legally represented)*

Your (your solicitor's) address

reference or contact name _____

contact telephone number _____

DX number _____

N161 Appellant's Notice (10.00)

1

Printed on behalf of The Court Service

| Section 3 | Respondent's name and address |

Respondent's name _____

Solicitor's name _____ *(if the respondent is legally represented)*

Respondent's (solicitor's) contact address

[ ] reference or contact name [ ]

contact telephone number [ ]

DX number [ ]

Details of other respondents are attached [ ] Yes [ ] No

| Section 4 | Time estimate for appeal hearing |

Do not complete if appealing to the Court of Appeal

| | Days | Hours | Minutes |

How long do you estimate it will take to put your appeal to the appeal court at the hearing? [ ][ ][ ]

Who will represent you at the appeal hearing? [ ] Yourself [ ] Solicitor [ ] Counsel

| Section 5 | Details of the order(s) or part(s) of order(s) you want to appeal |

Was the order you are appealing made as the result of a previous appeal? Yes [ ] No [ ]

Name of Judge [ ] Date of order(s) [ ]

If only part of an order is appealed, write out that part (or those parts)

[   ]

Was the case allocated to a track? Yes [ ] No [ ]

If Yes, which track was the case allocated to? [ ] small claims track [ ] fast track [ ] multi-track

Is the order you are appealing a case management order? Yes [ ] No [ ]